Counting
Up to
Christmas

Counting Up to Christmas

Twenty-Four Gifts from the Gospel of Luke

†

JENNIFER ELWOOD

For my husband, Tom.

Your unwavering support gave me
the treasured gift of love.

I am forever grateful.

Table of Contents

A Note from Jennifer

Dear Reader,

I am filled with joy over the opportunity to travel with you through the Gospel of Luke this Christmas season. For the past few years, the Lord revealed many gifts from Scripture to me as I sat at my kitchen table surrounded by Bibles, commentaries, and pages of notes. I cannot wait to share them with you.

My journey through the book of Luke each December began when I perused an article suggesting to read a chapter a day in December. This idea worked well for me. As a former speech pathologist, Luke's well-researched, scholarly accounts of the gospel and the early church in Acts appealed to my cerebral nature.

Because the book of Luke contains twenty-four chapters, the month ties up in a perfect bow. We begin December with the cry of our Savior and King born into poverty amongst the lowing of animals. On Christmas Eve, we hear the astonished cries from witnesses at an empty tomb. The timing is sheer perfection.

The writing of this study began after the one year I neglected my reading of Luke in December. That year I led an online Advent study for my church and was so busy I forgot to begin!

Around December 10th, I panicked when I realized how tough it would be to fit it in. The Holy Spirit used my mistake to 'nudge' me. That book idea I'd prayed about for years? It was time to write this Christmas practice of reading Luke into a Bible study to share with others. I asked the Lord when to begin, and felt Christmas music would sing its way into my summer playlist.

In June, after the insane pace required for the end of school year events with two school-aged children and a needy toddler in tow, we decided to go to Disney World. As we prepared to leave, the thought crossed my mind to begin writing, but I put it off. Little did I know the Lord had plans to surprise and encourage me.

Disney World is the happiest place on earth . . . and also super stressful at times. As we entertained a teenage boy and two younger girls, we completely wore ourselves out. On a day I planned more time at Magic Kingdom, the kids asked (a.k.a. whined) to go to Blizzard Beach. I reluctantly canceled our Fast Passes and got swim gear and sunblock ready for a water outing, fussing myself into a tizzy as we boarded the bus. As we entered the water-park, however, I could barely believe my ears.

Christmas music.

All day long, heaven-sent Christmas music piped into my brain. It washed over my heart and I became convinced: it was time to begin. I read Luke 1 that evening and nearly every day for a month. On July 25th, Christmas in July, I walked into a medical office and heard Christmas music—again. That night, I sat down and poured out the message from my heart to my laptop and wrote the first draft of Chapter One. The work had finally begun.

How to Use this Book

I originally intended for this book to be a more in-depth Bible study. However, I know how little time I have to study around Christmas, so this book works like a devotional with study components sprinkled through the chapters.

Each day, you're encouraged to read the chapter of Luke that corresponds to the day of the month. Just so you know, it takes about two-and-a-half hours to read the entire book of Luke. If you spread that over twenty-four days, it's not an exorbitant amount of reading time. You can do it!

Next, read the teaching for each day to open the gift from Scripture that Jesus offers. I've included a photo or work of art that is meant to enhance elements from each lesson. I have visited Israel twice and included several pictures from my collection as well as a few other images. For me, connecting to the place these events occurred brings an enlightening element to Bible reading. I hope it does for you, too.

Following the teaching, you're invited to pray, then spend a little time in "Christmas Quietude"—a state of stillness meant to engage us in deeper connection with the Lord. You'll find a suggested verse for meditation and some blank space to journal if you'd like.

Then, Christmas music! Each day concludes with a Christmas worship song. I make a suggestion and you may listen to whatever version suits your fancy.

If you'd like to access YouTube worship links, or a free journal that accompanies the e-book, you can find PDFs on my website at www.jenniferelwood.com. You are also invited to connect with others from December 1st to 25th in the Facebook group "Counting Up To Christmas: 24 Gifts from the Gospel of Luke" as well as on Instagram at @peacocksojourning. Both communities will receive daily worship links and community encouragement.

Lastly, you can keep track of your scripture gift opening progress in this book on page 13. If you miss a day, no worries. I understand the hectic nature of the season, and best of all, Jesus does, too. However, my hope and prayer is that your number one priority will be time in Scripture each day. Pretty please, read the gospel account first. If you're busier than usual this month, perhaps you could commit to early mornings or later evenings to ensure enough time. I highly recommend listening to the chapter via audio recording if you don't have the time to sit and read.

My ultimate hope for you this Christmas season is to resist panic and allow peace to persist. There is no better time to wrap ourselves in the words of Luke's finely detailed gospel and open the gifts presented to us. Each year at Christmastime, we have many gifts we can choose to offer and receive. However, the best gift is reading God's Word every day. Once opened, it will overflow to others around us because of the miraculous way He changes us. This provision from the Lord continues to give to me each time I open it and has transformed my heart.

Let's do Christmas differently this year. My prayer for us is that purposeful peace in Christ will descend, no matter the circumstances.

☐ December 1
☐ December 2
☐ December 3
☐ December 4

☐ December 5
☐ December 6
☐ December 7
☐ December 8

☐ December 9
☐ December 10
☐ December 11
☐ December 12

☐ December 13
☐ December 14
☐ December 15
☐ December 16

☐ December 17
☐ December 18
☐ December 19
☐ December 20

☐ December 21
☐ December 22
☐ December 25

☐ December 23
☐ December 24

This is my daughter, Ella Rose, demonstrating what prayer might have looked like on that day long ago. I asked her to imagine baby Jesus and this was her beautiful response.

Receive the Gift of Prayer

December

1

READ † **Luke 1**

CONTEMPLATE †

"And the whole multitude of the people were praying outside at the hour of incense."

—Luke 1:10, ESV

RECEIVE THE GIFT † Prayer

Have you ever missed seeing a wrapped package tucked into the layers of a Christmas tree? Or perhaps like the Red-Rider BB gun from one of my favorite Christmas movies, the gift was held back purposefully and revealed with great fanfare. The excitement of the morning waned and the floor was covered in a colorful mess of paper and boxes . . . but there was one last, special gift waiting just for you.

This is how I feel about Luke 1:10. It's sitting right in front of us, beautifully wrapped. It's not only something we want, but desperately need to open: the gift of *prayer*.

To understand the significance of this simple but powerful gift, let's open the scene where Luke 1 took place. Let's consider how that day may have looked as a woman in the crowd in Jerusalem more than 2,000 years ago.

I was up before the sun rose that morning in our simple home on the outskirts of Jerusalem. My family is among the faithful continuing to hope in the Lord, but 400 years have passed with no prophetic message in Israel. Our souls are dry. It was quiet in my home as I prepared for my family to rise, but across the city, the Temple bustled with activity. A family clan[1] within a division of about 5,000 priests[2] purified themselves and prepared for the day's tasks while I cooked breakfast.

I set out with children in tow, and we climbed up to the Temple just as the sun broke over the horizon. It wasn't just a few hundred people we were joining—the whole assemblage was present in prayer that day. We squeezed in and repetitively bowed in prayer.

Inside the Temple, the third lot of the day was cast to choose which priest would light the incense in the Holy Place[3]. Zechariah was the one chosen for this once-in-a-lifetime task. "The blessing of Heaven-sent bounty and prosperity"[4] was on its way.

Or was it? Suddenly we heard news whispered through the streets: the priest who offered the incense could not speak! Those passing on his gestured message told us he experienced a vision. We wondered what it could mean.

About six months later, rumors revealed that the elderly priest's wife Elizabeth was pregnant. The offering of incense, a representation of prayer, was the conduit to answer their prayer for a baby. We wondered: Could it be that this extraordinary child was the fulfillment of Isaiah's prophesy?

"A voice of one calling: 'In the wilderness prepare the way for the LORD; make straight in the desert a highway for our God." – Isaiah 40:3, NIV

Could it be that our hope in the Lord was not in vain? The one to precede the Messiah was here, and little did we know, Jesus was on His way. Devout prayer was not only a gift to Zechariah and Elizabeth, but also for us.

Is prayer just as important to us now as it was then? It should be. We need prayer in a desperate way. The Christmas season is wonderful, joyous, and highly anticipated every year. It is also particularly busy. The gatherings, decorating, baking, extra school, church, and community activities, and pressure to buy all the things can distract and unnerve us if we allow them to.

Instead of spending this season pressured by stress, let's daily ignite our internal incense and have intentional, unrushed prayer. Let's weave our words into rising praise and gratitude. From that place, we can find grace for others that would be impossible on our own.

 **PRAYER**

My soul sings praise to the Lord! I rejoice in You, Jesus. I am fortunate that You look at my mess and have kind thoughts of me. I am grateful that You, Lord, are holy and mighty. You are merciful to every person who ever lived. You are wonderful and strong and Your justice is perfect. Thank You for giving me a heart for the Church and for the land and people of Israel. I worship You and am grateful that You are helpful and wise. Thank You for sending Your Son so that all who believe will live with You forever. Amen!

CHRISTMAS QUIETUDE

In silence with the Lord, I encourage you to use the space below to compose a prayer to set the tone for this month. I used Mary's Magnificat from Luke 1:46-55 as my model. This lovely prayer sprang forth as she discovered her pregnancy and that of her cousin Elizabeth.

_____

_____

_____

_____

_____

_____

_____

_____

WORSHIP † *"My Soul Magnifies the Lord"*

May our souls magnify the Lord as we worship with this song of praise!

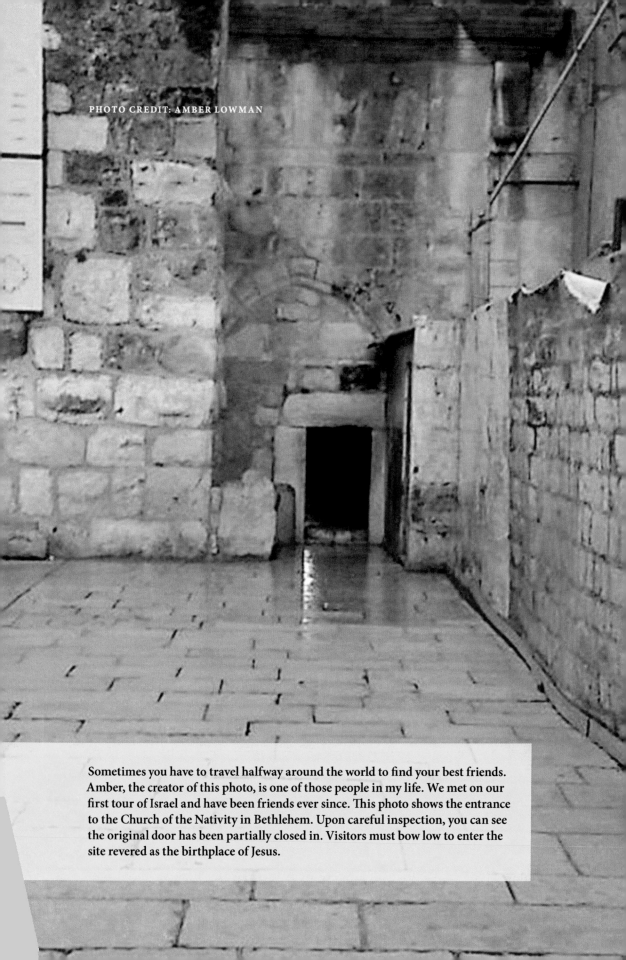

Sometimes you have to travel halfway around the world to find your best friends. Amber, the creator of this photo, is one of those people in my life. We met on our first tour of Israel and have been friends ever since. This photo shows the entrance to the Church of the Nativity in Bethlehem. Upon careful inspection, you can see the original door has been partially closed in. Visitors must bow low to enter the site revered as the birthplace of Jesus.

Receive the Gift of Jesus' Birth

December
2

READ † **Luke 2**

CONTEMPLATE †
"And she gave birth to her
firstborn son, and wrapped him
in swaddling cloths and laid
him in a manger; because there
was no place for them in the inn."
—Luke 2:7, ESV

RECEIVE THE GIFT † Jesus' Divine Birth

I love a good birth story, don't you? My experience of yearning and excitement during pregnancy and birth was a nine-month process of unwrapping the most tremendous gift imaginable. I could regale you with innumerable details of my son's birth as he was tediously unpacked over a crazy twenty-four-hour period from the nurturing, protective space he occupied for nine months. After much anticipation, I looked down on a Thursday night in December of 2004 at a most lavish gift: my sweet son.

Today, we will unwrap another birth story and encounter the gift found in a manger: *Jesus' divine birth.* Jesus' young, first-time parents eagerly awaited His birth. However, mankind anticipated this event for thousands of years before it happened. I absolutely love how the Bible shows us details about our coming Savior in every book.

I invite you to contemplate this gift by grabbing a Bible and your favorite pen. Let's write some of these verses down and embrace the hope ushered in by the joyous birth of Christ.

We start "In the beginning" . . .

Write down **Genesis 3:15**

_____

_____

_____

When God gave this prophecy to Adam and Eve, the guilty couple was covered in leaves and shame. Their expulsion from the perfect garden and the Lord's constant presence remains the saddest event in history.

But, it's not over. We see a glimmer of hope and future redemption in this verse. I read a commentary that stated, "A gracious promise is here made of Christ . . ."[5] So gracious indeed. God did not abandon His people. He provided the victory over sin in an unexpected way, a baby who claimed victory in battle against an evil serpent. A divine birth that would undo Satan.

Write down **Genesis 49:10**

_____

_____

_____

Let's trace Jesus' family line to His direct ancestor Jacob, grandson of Abraham. We glean more detail about the divine birth of Jesus as we witness Jacob offering a blessing to his son, Judah. He predicted the kingship of Jesus, complete with a scepter and ruler's staff. In Luke 2, we learn that Jesus' earthly father Joseph is a descendent of King David. A quick look at either genealogy of Jesus[6] shows us that David was from the line of Judah.

I don't think many people understood the divine birth with clarity. How could they? God brought His Son into the world in an unexpected way. The eternal King and hope of humanity arrived in the poverty of an animal stall.

I could imagine Elizabeth having an inkling of Jesus' identity. Perhaps she visited Mary after the birth of Jesus with a toy shaped like a scepter, offered with a little wink.

Write down **Micah 5:2**

_____

_____

_____

Micah prophesied in Israel around 700 years before Jesus' birth. He predicted the place where the gift of divine birth occurred, Bethlehem Ephrathah. I love how God, the ultimate ruler of the universe, did not bring His Son into the world with great fanfare. Jesus was born in a place "too little to be among the clans of Judah."[7] Out of the limelight, this simple locale witnessed the birth of the Messiah. What a humble beginning for the Son of God.

Write down **Isaiah 7:14**

_____

_____

_____

I like to imagine Mary, the only woman who experienced a divine, virgin birth, pondering this verse in her heart. Isaiah prophesied about her unusual reality 600 years before she lived.

I read an illuminating fact about the word "virgin" in a commentary. _Almah_, the original Hebrew word from Isaiah, referred to a young woman recently arrived at puberty and not sexually active[8]. The word fully wrapped up her physical status with her virtue and the high moral excellence of her character. It was to and through this teenage girl that our gift was originally delivered.

Write down **Isaiah 11:1**

_____

_____

_____

I read a beautiful quote about this verse: "The shining star has risen and the flower has grown from the root of Jesse – this is Christ."[9] This sprout of hope quietly and unceremoniously came into the world. Jesus came not as a conquering warrior, but with gentle love and grace. Truly, this divine birth is an exquisite gift for us to behold.

Let's take in one last glorious verse from Isaiah, a soul-refreshing testament of Jesus' character:

For a child is born to us,

† a son is given to us.

† The government will rest upon His shoulders.

† And he will be called:

† Wonderful Counselor, Mighty God,

† Everlasting Father, Prince of Peace. – Isaiah 9:6, NLT

 PRAYER

Lord, we praise You for the gift of Jesus' divine birth. We thank you for the account of our Savior, given over centuries so we can comprehend without a doubt: Jesus is Your Son. We remain grateful for His arrival to the world. Amen.

CHRISTMAS QUIETUDE

Spend a few moments meditating on the verses you wrote today. Ponder the gift brought to your life through the divine birth of Jesus.

_____

_____

_____

_____

_____

_____

_____

_____

_____

_____

_____

_____

_____

_____

_____

_____

WORSHIP † *"O Little Town of Bethlehem"*

Have gratitude for your Savior's divine birth in Bethlehem as you enjoy this Christmas classic.

Yardenit is a possible baptism site on the Jordan River. Isn't it refreshing? When I get to go next time, I'm not sure how I will resist jumping in!

PHOTO CREDIT: JENNIFER ELWOOD

Receive the Gift of Our True Father

December
3

READ † **Luke 3**

CONTEMPLATE †

"Now when all the people were baptized and when Jesus also had been baptized and was praying, the heavens were opened, and the Holy Spirit descended on him in bodily form, like a dove; and a voice came from heaven, 'You are my beloved Son; with you I am well pleased.'"

—Luke 3:21-22, ESV

RECEIVE THE GIFT † **Our True Father**

I get so excited for holiday gatherings. It is a joy for me to plan and attend these fun events. I enjoy decorating spaces in my home for relaxed conversation, baking memory-making foods like Aunt Dori's cookies, and attending parties set up with attentive detail.

One aspect of Christmas celebrations I love is the presence of family. My tribe truly blesses me. As we all know, however, sometimes family can be a source of aggravation that deflates our holiday cheer. For those times, we need to rely on today's gift, *our true Father*, to have peace in the midst of challenging relationships.

The tone of family hems in this chapter of Luke. We open with brothers ruling the land and a father-in-law and son-in-law[10] occupying roles of the high priesthood. The genealogy of Jesus summarizes this conclusion. However, we will view today's gift by peeling through the layers of family in the middle.

The baptism of Jesus beckons us to Luke 3:21, where cousin John presided over Jesus' baptism. Matthew 3:13-15 records their dialogue. Write down the conversation between John and Jesus.

John:

_____

_____

_____

Jesus:

_____

_____

_____

When I read John's incredulous response, I questioned how he refused Jesus. Then I realized John's purpose for baptism was repentance. Dunking his perfect cousin did not make sense to him. He knew Jesus all his life and surely noticed his cousin's sinless state.

Jesus' response was flawless. His inauguration into public ministry wasn't about repentance. "To fulfill all righteousness"[11] through baptism demonstrated approval from God. John understood righteousness and stepped forth in obedience.

God, our true Father, breathed a gift in words over the flowing water of the Jordan River. Perhaps you need to hear them today, written especially for you?

"You are my daughter, and you bring me great joy."

I long to hear words like these, particularly when I experience tangled emotions. I yearn to bring delight to others. Our amazing Father God wants to drop these words in our hearts like a lilting dove descending from the heavens. Will we open up enough to receive them?

As we prepare for Christmas, let's remember that time spent with our true Father fills us with contentment and enables us to process thorny feelings with grace. If we center our identity around this truth, we will have everything we need to process deepening relationships—and discontented people—in the midst of our celebrations.

PRAYER

Lord, thank You for being our true Father! We are grateful for the contentment we receive when we rest in You. Please help us remember Your truth and presence as we navigate our way through this month. Help our minds recollect words of Scripture when we need them to soothe our souls. In Your Son's precious name, Amen.

CHRISTMAS QUIETUDE

Let's engage our hearts and consider the gift of our true Father. Spend some time meditating on our verse in peace and quiet. Write down a remembrance from your quietude here.

_____

_____

_____

_____

_____

_____

_____

_____

WORSHIP † *"Hallelujah Chorus"*

As you listen to today's worship selection, imagine the majestic event of Jesus' baptism where Father, Son, and Holy Spirit were tangibly all in one place.

Me, with Bible in hand at the Nazareth Precipice.
I'm on the edge of the Jezreel Valley where many of
the Bible's heroes and villains traversed this land.
It is the location where Jesus will win the final battle
for freedom from sin. Can I get a hallelujah!?
(Revelation 16:14-16)

PHOTO CREDIT:KRISTIN ST. MARTIN

Receive the Gift of Freedom

December
4

READ † **Luke 4**

CONTEMPLATE †

"The Spirit of the Lord is on me, because he has anointed me to proclaim good news to the poor. He has sent me to proclaim freedom for the prisoners and recovery of sight for the blind, to set the oppressed free, to proclaim the year of the Lord's favor."

—Luke 4:18-19, NIV

RECEIVE THE GIFT † **Freedom in Jesus**

Do you have favorite Christmas jewelry? I save a shiny set of pearls for special occasions that my grandma purchased for me in San Francisco (because that's what you do there, she told me). I also have containers full of favorite Christmas decorations—glittery, colorful trinkets that elicit delightful memories as I place them in my home each December. However, all the extra effort that goes into adornment can frazzle me, too. When I allow myself to be weighed down with the responsibility of perfection I get exhausted, lose my temper, and quickly sound like a crazy harridan. This version of me does not match my lovely pearls or vintage angels.

When our tempers fly off the handle, we need to remember our ability to adorn our hearts, minds, and mouths with the decoration of peace that can be found in our gift today: *freedom in Jesus.*

Let's consider what it means to be a free person. A free person is someone who can say or do whatever they desire. It implies liberation; no one owns them. So, basically I can do whatever I want if I am free . . . awesome! I like to do what I feel like doing. But is that *true* freedom?

As believers in Christ, let's consider the Bible's definition of freedom. The truth is that in order to be truly free, we must be slaves of God.

Wait, what? How is that free?

The sad and unfortunate truth is that sin puts us in heavy shackles. I don't want shackles; they're cumbersome, uncomfortable, and ugly. I want pretty bracelets and pearl necklaces adorning me, thank you very much! So, how can we trade these nasty irons of slavery for something beautiful?

We see the adornment of freedom by looking at how Jesus dressed His words: with God's Word. When Jesus rebuffed the devil's repulsive handcuffs in the wilderness, His response was covered in jewels from God's Word. Later in His hometown synagogue, He unswervingly proclaimed the delightful truth of Scripture. His friends and family would attempt to crush the pearls of honesty He offered. He knew this, but He still offered it to them.

Friends, the simple but challenging truth is this: the key to releasing us from bondage is embellishing our minds, hearts, and speech with God's Word. When we purposefully tether ourselves to Jesus with the words of Scripture, we gain a position of strength, power, and beauty that is impossible on our own. His yoke anchors us with an exquisite necklace of love.

So, let's make the complicated simple by taking practical steps to adorn ourselves with the words of God. Paul, a later disciple of Jesus, fully understood the mastership of Jesus as our true freedom. Write some of his wise words below.

Ephesians 3:12

_____

_____

_____

Galatians 5:1

_____

_____

_____

2 Corinthians 3:17

_____

_____

_____

Romans 6:22

_____

_____

_____

PRAYER

Master, we praise You for the freedom You offer through belief in your Son. Thank You for granting us perfect emancipation with Jesus' sacrifice on the cross. Please help us to spread the gift of freedom in You to the people around us. We need boldness to spread the gospel message. We want to represent You and the freedom You offer well. Amen.

CHRISTMAS QUIETUDE

For your time of peace today, read aloud the verses of freedom you wrote down. Spend some time meditating through them. Use the space below to write anything the Lord places on your heart in the quiet.

_____

_____

_____

_____

_____

_____

_____

_____

_____

_____

_____

_____

_____

_____

WORSHIP † *"Mary Did You Know?"*

Let's consider the presence of Jesus' mother at the Synagogue scene. Imagine her heart swell as her son announced what she already knew, that He would set captives free. Envision her heart again, but this time broken, as the brawling people, likely her own family included, tried to end Jesus' life. Let's ponder as we worship with this Christmas song.

Mary Did You Know

Mary did you know that your baby boy would one day walk on water?
Mary did you know that your baby boy would save our sons and daughters?
Did you know that your baby boy has come to make you new?
This child that you've delivered, will soon deliver you

Mary did you know that your baby boy will give sight to a blind man?
Mary did you know that your baby boy will calm a storm with his hand?
Did you know that your baby boy has walked where angels trod?
When you kiss your little baby, you kiss the face of God

Mary did you know? Mary did you know? Mary did you know?

Mary did you know? Mary did you know? Mary did you know?

The blind will see, the deaf will hear, the dead will live again
The lame will leap, the dumb will speak, the praises of the lamb

Mary did you know that your baby boy is Lord of all creation?
Mary did you know that your baby boy would one day rule the nations?
Did you know that your baby boy is heaven's perfect lamb?
That sleeping child you're holding is the great I am

Mary did you know? Mary did you know? Mary did you know?

Mary did you know? Mary did you know? Mary did you know? Oh

Mary did you know?

We don't know the exact location this miracle occurred, but we know Jesus preached and healed in the Decapolis. (Mark 5:20) Bet She'an is one of these ten cities. The spectacular ruins give us insight into the places Jesus traveled. This city witnessed the death of the first King of Israel, Saul, (1 Chronicles 10) and the healing power of our true, everlasting King, Jesus.

Receive the Gift of Healing

December
5

READ † **Luke 5**

CONTEMPLATE †

"And Jesus stretched out his hand
and touched him, saying, 'I will;
be clean.' And immediately the
leprosy left him."

—Luke 5:13, ESV

RECEIVE THE GIFT † Healing

Have you ever received such an amazing gift on Christmas morning that you snapped pics and posted to social media with wrapped presents still nestled under the tree? Have you ever had a video camera ready when a loved one opened something you knew they really wanted? My digital files contain captured moments like these.

When I consider the leper in today's reading, I find myself wishing Jesus had the latest smartphone way back then. I can imagine the sweet smile on His face as He captured the moment. As we receive this same gift, *healing*, imagine the love bomb dropped as He uttered, "You are clean."

Let's take a step back in time, put ourselves in tattered first-century sandals, and walk through a leper's perspective of healing.

*I've been leprous for years. Living on the outskirts of town in torn
clothes, dejected and in immense pain, I yelled "unclean" to anyone*

approaching[12]. Life is utterly miserable with no cure in sight. This disease attacked my peripheral nervous system; numb hands and feet are my daily reality. Painful, tumor-like sores cover my entire body[13]. I realize that without a miracle, I will NEVER heal.

But then, I hear the whispered rumors of a man who banished demons and healed the sick. I dare to hope for this torturous malady to disappear. And then, I hear Jesus is coming! Instead of crying out "unclean" as He passes by, new words come: "Lord, if you will, you can make me clean."[14]

My hope was not in vain. He restored my sensation, the scales dropped from my skin, and the refreshment of Jesus' healing washed over me.

But it isn't over. My next job, assigned by my Savior and curer, is to visit Jerusalem and accomplish full rehabilitation. Let's go! It took more than a week to gather the necessary components and walk to Jerusalem. I must bring four items to present to the priests:

1. *Cedar, one of the tallest trees, symbolizing the height of pride.*

2. *Hyssop, a low-growing wildflower, demonstrating the humility I need to recover.*

3. *Scarlet wool that binds these two cleansing plants, symbolizing that I am purified and healed.*

4. *Two sparrows to represent a possible cause of my leprosy, slander, with their "constant twitter." According to my Jewish culture, gossip caused this ailment.[15]*

Once in Jerusalem, with a red-wrapped cleansing bouquet and two little birds in hand, I walk uphill to the Temple. (I want to run . . . I'm SO close!) I make my way through various courtyards and into the Court of Women. I purify myself in a cleansing pool, a mikveh, and arise from full immersion reinvigorated. Then, my heart bursting in anticipation, I approach the Leper's Chamber. I witness the killing of one bird. Then the priest takes the living bird, dips it in the blood from the sacrifice, and sprinkles me seven times. The cacophony of the terrified bird pierces my soul, and I realize the imminent relief of renewal. As the living bird is released, I experience a new reality of recovery. The gift of healing, given to me by Jesus Himself, has been fully opened.

As I meditate on Jesus' healing power in my life, I spill tears. Because of His sacrifice on the cross, we can now approach the throne of God to simply ask for healing without complicated procedures. Praise the Lord! Releasing pride and bowing low in humility are not the easiest tasks. But pursuing this posture, even in an imperfect way, can enable us to say, "Jesus healed me." His blood shed on the cross covers us, symbolized by the sprinkling of the sacrificed bird's blood, which fully opens this gift.[16] Through the cross, we obtain freedom to spread our wings and fly fully healed.

PRAYER

Lord, we praise You for healing us! We are thankful for the wounds You've restored. Please expose painful areas that need recovery. We require Your help to fully receive the gift of healing You offer. In Jesus' name, Amen.

CHRISTMAS QUIETUDE

Spend a little time today praising Jehovah Rapha, God our healer. Consider how God repairs the painful places in our lives. Write a note of gratitude in the space below.

_____

_____

_____

_____

_____

_____

_____

WORSHIP † *"Light of the World"*

Let's be grateful that in a sea of hurt, the Light of World is here.

Mount Arbel, from the top looking out towards the Golan Heights. The Sea of the Galilee is on the right. This outlook helps me envision Jesus the Shepherd leading His followers and redefining faith through this exquisite landscape.

Receive the Gift of Reconciliation

READ † Luke 6

CONTEMPLATE †

"But I say to you who hear,
Love your enemies, do good to
those who hate you, bless those
who curse you, pray for those
who abuse you."

—Luke 6:27-28, ESV

RECEIVE THE GIFT † Reconciliation

We continue our uphill climb, counting toward the pinnacle of this miraculous season. Getting tired yet? So much preparation goes into this month, bringing great joy as well as weariness. I believe that in order to truly celebrate this month, we need a firm stepping stone—the gospel! As we read God's Word each day, we place immovable stones under our feet that make the trek possible.

We can, however, lose our footing at times. Relationships can easily become stumbling blocks. We tread rocky, unstable ground when we hold grudges. I am guilty of allowing rocks in the climbing boots of my soul to remain instead of taking the time to clear them out. Can you relate?

Let's consider today's verse. Jesus gives us wise, relational instruction. As we open today's gift of *reconciliation*, these words have the power to transform us as we consider how to love people well.

I want to virtually take you to Mount Arbel on the northwest shore of the Sea of Galilee. It is breathtakingly beautiful. An encounter there will provide the insight we need to open our gift today.

Imagine we're sitting next to each other on the cushy seats of a luxury tour bus. We zoom toward the place which is Jesus' ministry home, the Sea of Galilee. The bus stops and an easy hike awaits from the parking lot. Our hearts on overload, we reach the top and see the shimmering, clear blue lake. Jesus walked on that water! We hear our guide over the portable mic and learn that we stand in a possible location of the Sermon on the Plain from Luke 6.

We look out at the plateau and see the peaceful grazing pasture, a pleasant seating arrangement for the many who followed and heard Jesus speak those astounding words. Our pastoral scene ends as we descend to the bus.

This relaxed encounter did not represent the words Jesus spoke. His words challenged His audience by radically redefining Jewish cultural practices. During a time when people practiced eye-for-an-eye retribution, Jesus announced the importance of loving one's enemies.

This controversial, thought-provoking message is better represented by my friend Ilene Gerardi's encounter with Mount Arbel. She, like Jesus' early devotees, experienced a climb from the base, not a relaxed stroll from the parking spot. She shared it was a technical, nerve-wracking climb. Jesus' followers remained undeterred. Healing radiated from Him[17], which likely fueled their initial impetus to follow. They willed themselves to make the difficult climb to be in His presence and hear His words. Little did they know that Jesus intended to redefine their concepts of relationship and reconciliation.

Imagine sitting on that rocky plain among the gathered audience that surrounded Jesus as He taught the importance of caring for people who mistreated you. Jesus took watered down, mishandled rules and refreshed His followers with full, kingdom-informed truth. This teaching is bold and so loving. Standing on the firm foundation of the high plateau, we can feel the Word of Jesus drop the gift of reconciliation into our hearts.

Do you need to open the gift of reconciliation today? At times, this gift can seem as if it's wrapped in layers of packing tape. We find it difficult and cumbersome to open. We need to continually ask the Lord for help to accomplish this task. As we climb the heights to encounter Jesus, we also need to be humble. Jesus truly desires this in our relationships: the healing of your heart *and* theirs. Perhaps it is time to give in an exorbitant way, by praying for challenging people and seeking ways to be a blessing to them. As you do, imagine Jesus with a pocket knife, cutting open the box to reveal the splendid gift of reconciliation at the center.

Gracious Father, we praise You for the gift of reconciliation. We confess our wrongdoings. We plead for the humility required to make things right. Please guide our steps to help us receive forgiveness and reconciliation. Help us to be bold even when it is difficult. In Jesus' name, Amen.

CHRISTMAS QUIETUDE

Take some time in the quiet and meditate on today's verse. Prepare to act in obedience and fully receive the gift of reconciliation that God has in store for you. Write down a meaningful thought from your quietude here.

_____

_____

_____

_____

_____

_____

_____

_____

WORSHIP † *"Go Tell It On the Mountain"*

Enjoy this wonderful song as you contemplate sharing the gift of reconciliation from the rooftops!

That is me, a faith-filled woman on a mission to see her Savior's hometown. Kfar Nahum is the Hebrew name of this place. *Kfar* means village and *Nahum* means comforter. (My Hebrew teacher would be proud that I'm telling you this!) How perfect that Jesus' ministry home would have such a name.

PHOTO CREDIT: KRISTIN ST. MARTIN

Receive the Gift of Faith

December
7

READ † Luke 7

CONTEMPLATE †

"When Jesus heard these things, he marveled at him, and turning to the crowd that followed him, said, 'I tell you, not even in Israel have I found such faith.'"

—Luke 7:9, ESV

"And he said to the woman, 'Your faith has saved you; go in peace.'"

—Luke 7:50, ESV

RECEIVE THE GIFT † **Faith**

It's usually around this time in December that I feel disheartened as I witness people experience Christmas without Jesus. The world's account of this season with commercialism, the draining of bank accounts, and the inevitable stress that follows saddens me. I get overwhelmed with the ramped-up onslaught of commercials for every toy and gadget imaginable well before we carve the Thanksgiving turkey.

I need today's gift of *faith* to help me focus on the right thing this month: *Jesus.* I'm guessing you do, too.

We have two excellent examples of bold faith that bolster us in this chapter. First, let's march in formation toward the story of the Centurion.

This man commanded 100 soldiers[18] in the Roman army and could easily frighten us with his armor and power. But he is a foreigner armed with kindness who engaged the local population. They clearly respect him. When I consider him, I don't picture a hardened soldier, but a strong, humble man who decided a long time ago to do the right thing even when it wasn't easy. I see a softened, servant heart ready to accept Jesus. He reminds me of my husband. Tom is a businessman with a firm attitude who can intimidate. However, he possesses humility and *really* loves Jesus. His servant attitude toward others softens his edges.

In both men, I see the kind of faith I want to have. The kind that says, "I may have power, but I need Jesus more." The sort of boldness that tells Jesus His concrete, physical presence is unnecessary because they truly believe He has the power to accomplish what He desires.

Now let's examine another example of audacious faith: the "sinful woman." When an event in the Bible piques my curiosity, I like to read it in a few different versions. I definitely want to know more about a woman who comes uninvited to a dinner party and uses her hair to rub expensive oil on a man's feet!

As we take in her description, we notice a few things. She's described in two different paraphrases as the "town harlot"[19] and "a woman of ill repute."[20] We can discern an awful, marked past.

The word "woman" in the original Greek implied her married status.[21] The word used for "sinner" was a contemptuous Aramaic word, referencing the class of transgressor despised by strict Jews.[22] Down and out and with nothing to lose, she showed up: brave, unannounced, and unafraid. What an example of embraced faith in our Savior.

 **PRAYER**

Jesus, thank You for the gracious gift of faith in our lives! We praise You that belief in Your Son exists not by our own power, but through Yours. We pray our example of faith would encourage others. Please help us hear Your heartbeat on how to demonstrate this. We totally rely on You, Lord. Prepare the hearts of those around us who need to experience Your glory. In Jesus' name, Amen.

CHRISTMAS QUIETUDE

Spend some time in silence with the author and perfecter of your faith. Seek Him. Delight in Him. Prepare yourself to glorify the Lord through faith-filled action this season like never before. Write down one person you plan to share your faith with.

_____

_____

_____

_____

_____

_____

_____

_____

_____

WORSHIP † *"O Come, All Ye Faithful"*

Time to Praise Him, all ye faith-full . . .

As you look at this photo, imagine the strain in your hand as you reach out with determined trust in the healing wings of Jesus. (Special thanks to my dad who provided the feet of Jesus.

PHOTO CREDIT: JENNIFER ELWOOD

Receive the Gift of Determined Trust

December

8

READ † **Luke 8**

CONTEMPLATE †
"And he said to her, 'Daughter, your faith has made you well; go in peace.'"

—Luke 8:48, ESV

RECEIVE THE GIFT † **Determined Trust**

Do you treasure sledding as a winter pastime? We do, and a sledding hill blesses our property. When the weather creates the sparkle of morning frost, the kids begin to wonder when snow will follow. Once blanketed with a thick layer of fluffy white, we climb the hill in endless repetition and enjoy the rush back down.

One year, my oldest child Mitchell wanted to try a steeper, tree-laden slope on the other end of the property. I agreed to scope it out, and one run appeared safe. As he began the descent, I watched as his head barreled down toward a slightly bent tree in his path. I screamed for him to bail out, but he didn't hear me. Then a crazy thing happened. As his little noggin approached the trunk of the tree, his sled seemed to be pushed by an invisible hand. He narrowly avoided a trip to the hospital (or worse). As I look back on that event, I realize my need for our gift today: *determined trust*.

At any given moment, it's a challenge to fully trust the Lord with every aspect of our lives. How often have devastating events or misplaced trust in people brought an edge of suspicion into your relationship with Jesus? The choice for determined trust needs continual re-evaluation as we move our eyes off the world and focus our gaze firmly on the Lord.

To me, determined trust means never giving up on the pursuit of God. We can trust that God is good, loving, and will act according to His will to shape us into the image of His Son. The ability to trust God enough to say in any situation "not my will, but yours, be done,"[23] is an amazing gift indeed.

So, let's reach out for our Savior's hand and get our grit on. We will don tattered, red-stained rags and peer into the life of the bleeding woman to help us open the gift so wonderfully demonstrated in our reading today.

I am unclean and unwelcome. Living on the outskirts of town for twelve years,[24] I spent all my money on doctors with no answers. Then rumors of Jesus' healing power met my ears. I replaced the message of the world that said, "Healing is impossible" with "If I touch even His garments, I will be made well."[25] Trust in Him ignited. Determined, I decided to press into the crowd in hopes of receiving healing unnoticed.

But I learned something that day: Jesus exists to glorify His Father through our trust. He cannot allow power to release in silence. Looking up from the ground with the dust of His fringe on my fingers, I met His compassionate gaze as He asked, "Who was it that touched me?"[26]

As I hear Jesus pronounce me well, He is interrupted. A child is dead. Someone else in the crowd waited on Jesus with determined faith too: Jairus.

My newly healed body imagines Jairus' wife at home, weeping over their dying daughter. I fervently pray Jesus will deliver a miracle for this family, too. I hear later, through the grapevine, the little girl is alive!

As I contemplate my miracle, the words of Malachi 4:2 play in my mind: "But for you who fear my name, the sun of righteousness will rise with healing in its wings."[27] These words resonate in my heart with the sensation of healing power I experienced when I touched the tassels on the edge of His prayer shawl.[28] Did my determined trust have the power to fulfill this prophecy?

We can learn so much from these stories today. Life can be hard. Perhaps, like me, you need your confidence in the Lord reignited. Are you weary of praying for someone who seems unlikely to change? Maybe you're dealing with discouragement in another area of your life—an unwanted diagnosis, parenting difficulties, or the calling to a task that seems impossible. May we allow the Lord to give us the determination we need to trust Him, no matter our circumstances.

PRAYER

Lord, as we experience what this Christmas season brings, we praise You for the inner workings of Your Word in our lives. Thank You for supplying every-thing we need to have determined faith and persistence of relationship with You. Please help us display bold, tenacious faith to those around us as we celebrate the birth of Your Son, Jesus. Amen.

CHRISTMAS QUIETUDE

In the quiet today, meditate on our verse. Write down a remembrance of something you sought from the Lord with determined faith.

_____

_____

_____

_____

_____

_____

_____

WORSHIP † *"Love Came Down"*

Love came down through the healing wings of Jesus. Worship the Lord with determined faith while you listen to this song today.

As I was writing this book, my niece studied Luke for a school project. When I saw her creation for this chapter, I knew I needed to share it with you.

Receive the Gift of Generosity

December 9

READ † **Luke 9**

CONTEMPLATE †

"Taking the five loaves and the two fish and looking up to heaven, he gave thanks and broke them. Then he gave them to the disciples to distribute to the people."

– Luke 9:16, NIV

RECEIVE THE GIFT † **Generosity**

Memories of waking up to a tree flush with gifts underneath bring me great delight. Other than the time as a teen when my big gift was an electric razor for my legs that I opened in front of everyone with 13-year-old horror, receiving items picked out especially for me is a highlight. How do you feel when you rise Christmas morning and see your name on packages that are a complete surprise?

In today's reading, the surprising gift of generosity strikes me, in both the words of Jesus as well as the nourishment He provides to the 5,000 men and uncounted women and children.

The feeding of the 5,000 is an event that marks Jesus' ministry style and is one of the rare stories told in all four gospel accounts. Preceding this crowd-pleasing meal, Jesus received the terrible announcement that Herod the Tetrarch killed Jesus' cousin, John. Obviously distraught, he leaves, but the people won't leave him alone.

Let's view this event from the perspective of a woman in the crowd:

It was a normal day at home. My family and I were busy performing our daily tasks. Then we were interrupted—we heard that Jesus was not far away. Jesus! We'd never seen Him before, but we'd heard of the miracles. I hastily grabbed the kids and headed out the door toward the Sea of Galilee. I didn't have to wonder where to go; we simply followed the flow of the crowd toward the lake. We marveled at the amount of people present. We hadn't seen a gathering of that magnitude since our last trek to Jerusalem.

We joined the throng of people shuffling toward the boat for their turn with Jesus, the man who is known to be so generous with His healing power. Our neighbors approached, full of excitement, and shared their healing miracle with us. Then Jesus left the boat. We all followed Him to a remote place—we just couldn't help ourselves. Our tummies began to twinge with hunger, but we couldn't leave. The event was way too exciting!

Jesus finally stopped walking, surrounded by many people in the middle of nowhere. I panicked a little. My kids and I didn't have any food with us. I began to wonder if the grass was tasty.

But Jesus somehow saw our appetites, both physical and spiritual. All of a sudden, groups received orders to sit down. Time passed, then our group received a basket FULL of fish and bread. We all wondered, "Where in the world did this come from?" So grateful for the generous gift, we ate the delicious food until we'd all had enough. Over 5,000 people attended the impromptu gathering, and Jesus fed us all. We were all astonished by Jesus' amazing power, love, and generosity.

Amazingly generous indeed. As we consider the deeper meaning of Christmas, let's turn our thoughts toward how to pass this gift of a generous Lord to others. We have eternal life through the sacrifice of His Son. This fact is a gift worth sharing with everyone!

 **PRAYER**

Lord, we are SO thankful for the many gifts You have given us through Your generosity. Please tenderize our hearts to receive You, and help us generously give to others from the overflow. In Jesus' name, Amen.

CHRISTMAS QUIETUDE

In the silence we carve out for ourselves today, consider the Lord's generosity toward you. Write down an event when you experienced this gift.

_____

_____

_____

_____

_____

_____

_____

_____

_____

_____

_____

WORSHIP † *"How Many Kings"*

We don't need to wonder how many earthly kings would be as generous and Jesus—the answer is none. Let's enjoy this Christmas worship song today.

I found no work of art that fully captured the scene
of Mary, Martha, and Jesus, so we re-created it.
I hope this draws you into the reality of the moment.
Mary is thoughtfully portrayed by my daughter
Carol Anne, and Martha's explosive personality is
depicted by my niece Gracie Weber, who provided
the art for the previous chapter.

Receive the Gift of Fully Present Relationships

December 10

READ † Luke 10

CONTEMPLATE †
"'Martha, Martha,' the Lord answered, 'you are worried and upset about many things, but few things are needed— or indeed only one. Mary has chosen what is better and it will not be taken away from her.'"

—Luke 10:41-42, NIV

RECEIVE THE GIFT † **Fully Present Relationships**

Don't you just love Christmas parties? I certainly do—both planning and attending them. The best part for me is the one-on-one connection cultivated with people I love. We put away phones, the kids play, and the adults catch up . . . which provides the time needed to open today's gift, *fully present relationships.*

We see the layers of this gift unwrapped between Jesus and the beloved sisters, Mary and Martha. An examination of the original language shows amazing depth that English translations don't quite capture. Let's be word nerds today and pay attention to the deeper meaning we find.

Jesus sets the scene, teaching in Mary and Martha's home as preparations to feed Him and His entourage are underway. We see Mary, as the original Greek states, sitting beside Jesus.[29] She was right at His feet in the midst of His followers—a very favored position. At that time, the religious education of women focused on laws that centered around the care of the household.[30] Most women could only dream of being this close to Jesus. She was living out this gift of relationship so beautifully.

I wish we could continue this Hallmark card-worthy scene as is. However, the tranquility wasn't to last, because . . .

Here comes Martha.

This peaceful scene abruptly ended. The original language describing Martha is marked by an infusion of anxiety. She was distracted and troubled greatly.[31] The word used to describe her approach to Jesus indicates it was "abrupt"[32] as she rushed into the room looking for her sister. Then, she asked Jesus if He was *melei*, or anxious[33] about her sister's lack of regard for the preparations happening full-force in the kitchen.

For a moment, put yourself in her place. Many people at her home awaited a meal. We can hardly blame Martha for freaking out. Perhaps she had prior notice that Jesus was coming, perhaps not. When I have more than a few people over for an elaborate meal, I make lists a day or two in advance so I can complete most of the tasks before they come through the door. Even then, it can get stressful.

Of course, Jesus definitely was not stressed. He responded in such a sweet way and offered her a stress-less response.

"Martha, Martha," He said.

Jesus described her as over-anxious[34] and disturbed.[35] He would not remove Mary from her slice of heaven no matter how indignant her sister was feeling. I love how He so kindly and firmly dealt with Martha's apprehension and affirmed Mary's desire to be with Him.

We don't want to be too hard on Martha. The Gospel account of this story ends and we aren't privy to what happens next. If I were Martha, I would likely be holding back tears as I returned to the kitchen.

But the story doesn't end there. If we hop over to the Gospel of John, we experience these sisters a little further along in time. We see Martha's belief in Jesus has gone from head to heart and *she gets it.* Liz Curtis Higg's podcast illuminated this point to me[36] and I want to share it with you. In John 11:1-44, the sisters' brother Lazarus died. Four days passed and Jesus hadn't come. I can see Martha, eyes freshly brimming with tears every time she thought, "Jesus, Lord, if you had been here, my brother would not have died."[37]

Once Martha heard Jesus was on His way, she left her tasks behind in pursuit of a fully present relationship. During the discourse that followed, she received Jesus' statement, "I am the resurrection and the life. Whoever believes in me, though he die, yet shall he live, and everyone who lives and believes in me shall never die. Do you believe this?"[38] Then she declared, "Yes Lord; I believe that you are the Christ, the Son of God, who is coming into the world."[39] I mean, wow! You go, girl! Following this story to its end, we witness the fully opened gift of relationship flourish in the lives of both sisters.

We have so much to learn from these women who were blessed to grace the pages of the Bible. I hope that as the Christmas season continues, you carve out wonderful times of fully present relationships with Jesus and others.

PRAYER

Lord, we celebrate that You desire close knit, fully present relationships with us. Thank You that Jesus' connection to the women we experience in Scripture is available to us today. We pray that our pursuit of relationship with Jesus will not fade but continue strong. In Jesus' name, Amen.

CHRISTMAS QUIETUDE

During today's silence, ask Jesus to uncover anything that is getting in the way of a connection-driven, fully present relationship with Him. Write down something meaningful from your quietude in the space below.

_____

_____

_____

_____

_____

_____

_____

_____

_____

_____

_____

_____

_____

_____

_____

WORSHIP † *"Noel"*

As you continue to ponder your sacred connection with Jesus, come and see what God has done.

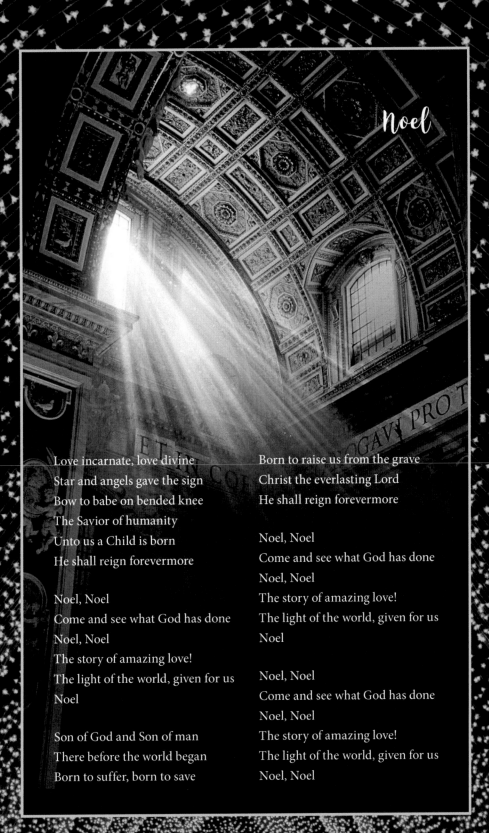

Noel

Love incarnate, love divine
Star and angels gave the sign
Bow to babe on bended knee
The Savior of humanity
Unto us a Child is born
He shall reign forevermore

Noel, Noel
Come and see what God has done
Noel, Noel
The story of amazing love!
The light of the world, given for us
Noel

Son of God and Son of man
There before the world began
Born to suffer, born to save

Born to raise us from the grave
Christ the everlasting Lord
He shall reign forevermore

Noel, Noel
Come and see what God has done
Noel, Noel
The story of amazing love!
The light of the world, given for us
Noel

Noel, Noel
Come and see what God has done
Noel, Noel
The story of amazing love!
The light of the world, given for us
Noel, Noel

In 2018, I went to Joppa with Kristin St. Martin. Not to run . . . but to engage. We read the book of Jonah on the shore. These pages of Jonah in my Bible have a bit of water damage. When we were there, "the Lord hurled a great wind upon the sea." (Jonah 1:4 ESV) Waves came up over the sea wall and splashed us, resulting in laughter from the people around us. We saw the event as a tangible reminder from the Lord of the biblical history that took place there.

PHOTO CREDIT: JENNIFER ELWOOD

Receive the Gift of the Inspired Word

December 11

READ † Luke 11

CONTEMPLATE †

"When the crowds were increasing, he began to say, 'This generation is an evil generation. It seeks for a sign, but no sign will be given to it except the sign of Jonah. For as Jonah became a sign to the people of Nineveh, so will the Son of Man be to this generation. . . . and behold, something greater than Jonah is here.'"

—Luke 11:29-30, 32b, ESV

RECEIVE THE GIFT † **The Inspired Word**

Have you ever opened a gift that was a bit of a puzzle? The gift today, *The Inspired Word*, hinges on Jesus revealing that He is the sign of Jonah. It was challenging to discern what Jonah, the grumpy prophet, and Jesus, the perfect God-with-us, had in common. The strangely-shaped package came covered in question mark printed wrapping paper and took me the summer of 2019 to peel open.

What I found within was a treasure trove of shiny, golden Scripture. The key that unlocked the glittery center was this: Every word of the second chapter of Jonah exists in other areas of Scripture. When we see so many words of the Bible working together harmoniously, it reveals the perfection of God and His Word. Consequently, if we truly believe that Jesus is God, we can trust these divinely inspired words from Jonah are His. The power of the Holy Spirit living in us reveals the truth of God's Word. The bottom line is that the Bible is magnificently perfect.

Whew! I know it's a lot to take in. Without another word from me, read through this account from Scripture yourself. Let the words of God, revealed partly in the belly of a great fish and the rest throughout the Bible, wash over your hearts and anchor the firm truth of today's Inspired Word gift.

"Then Jonah prayed to the LORD his God from the belly of the fish, saying,

'I called out to the LORD, out of my distress, and he answered me;	*"I called on your name, O LORD, from the depths of the pit;"* **Lamentations 3:55, NIV**
out of the belly of Sheol I cried,'	*"Out of my distress I called on the LORD; the LORD answered me and set me free."* **Psalm 118:5, ESV**
and you heard my voice." **Jonah 2:1-2, ESV**	*"You have heard my voice, "Do not hide Your ear from my prayer for relief, From my cry for help."* **Lamentations 3:56, NASB**
"You hurled me into the depths, into the very heart of the seas, and the currents swirled about me;	*"You have put me in the lowest pit, in the darkest depths. Your wrath lies heavily on me; you have overwhelmed me with all your waves."* **Psalm 88:6-7, NIV**
all your waves and breakers swept over me." **Jonah 2:3, NIV**	*"Deep calls to deep at the roar of your waterfalls; all your breakers and your waves have gone over me."* **Psalm 42:7, ESV**
"Then I said, 'I am driven away from your sight;	*"In panic I cried out, "I am cut off from the LORD!" But you heard my cry for mercy and answered my call for help."* **Psalm 31:22, NLT**
yet I shall again look upon your holy temple.'" **Jonah 2:4, ESV**	*"if they pray toward this Temple and acknowledge your name and turn from their sins"* **I Kings 8:35b, NLT**
"The engulfing waters threatened me,	*"the waters closed over my head, and I thought I was about to perish."* **Lamentations 3:54, NIV**
the deep surrounded me;	*"Save me, O God! For the waters have come up to my neck."* **Psalm 69:1, ESV**

seaweed was wrapped around my head at the roots of the mountains.

"Following Jewish burial custom, they wrapped Jesus' body with
the spices in long sheets of linen cloth."
John 19:40, NLT

I went down to the land whose bars closed upon me forever; yet you brought up my life from the pit, O LORD my God."
Jonah 2:5-6, NIV

"who redeems your life from the pit and crowns you with love and compassion,"
Psalm 103:4, NIV

"When my life was fainting away, I remembered the LORD, and my prayer came to you, into your holy temple."
Jonah 2:7, ESV

"Then the priests and the Levites arose and blessed the people,
and their voice was heard, and their prayer came to his holy habitation in heaven."
2 Chronicles 30:27, ESV

"Those who cling to worthless idols

"I hate those who worship worthless idols. I trust in the LORD." **Psalm 31:6, NLT**

turn away from God's love for them.

"for my people have committed two evils: they have forsaken me, the fountain of living waters, and hewed out cisterns for themselves, broken cisterns that can hold no water." **Jeremiah 2:13, ESV**

But I, with shouts of grateful praise, will sacrifice to you.
What I have vowed I will make good.

"Make thankfulness your sacrifice to God, and keep the vows you made to the Most High."
Psalm 50:14, NLT

I will say, 'Salvation comes from the Lord.' "
Jonah 2:8-9, NIV

"Salvation belongs to the LORD; your blessing be on your people! Selah" **Psalm 3:8, ESV**

Yes, yes, yes! Salvation, through Jesus, belongs to the Lord. Let's fully embrace the opening of this gift and the blessing that results.

 **PRAYER**

Lord, thank You for the gift of Inspired Word through the sign of Jonah. Thank You for Jesus, the forever-living sign of Jonah, who gave us the gift of eternal life through faith. We give You gratitude that salvation belongs to You, and that Your blessings are on Your people! Amen.

CHRISTMAS QUIETUDE

Choose one Scripture from the list above and meditate on it. Write down a remembrance from your quietude below.

_____

_____

_____

_____

_____

_____

_____

_____

_____

_____

_____

_____

_____

_____

_____

_____

WORSHIP † *"How Great Thou Art"*

Let's praise God for His greatness. I hope you are as grateful for His Inspired Word today as I am!

How Great Thou Art

O Lord, my God, when I in awesome wonder
Consider all the worlds Thy Hands have made
I see the stars, I hear the rolling thunder
Thy power throughout the universe displayed
Then sings my soul, my Saviour God, to Thee
How great Thou art, how great Thou art
Then sings my soul, my Saviour God, to Thee
How great Thou art, how great Thou art
And when I think of God, His Son not sparing
Sent Him to die, I scarce can take it in
That on the Cross, my burden gladly bearing
He bled and died to take away my sin
Then sings my soul, my Saviour God, to Thee
How great Thou art, how great Thou art
Then sings my soul, my Saviour God, to Thee
How great Thou art, how great Thou art
When Christ shall come with shout of acclamation
And lead me home, what joy shall fill my heart
Then I shall bow with humble adoration
And then proclaim, my God, how great Thou art
Then sings my soul, my Saviour God, to Thee
How great Thou art, how great Thou art
Then sings my soul, my Saviour God, to Thee
How great Thou art, how great Thou art

At the far right of this photo, we see the Western Wall. The sky was full with crescent-shaped swifts flitting to and from their nesting sites.

Receive the Gift of God's Care

December
12

READ † **Luke 12**

CONTEMPLATE †
"Fear not little flock, for it is
your Father's good pleasure
to give you the kingdom."
—Luke 12:32, ESV

RECEIVE THE GIFT † **God's Care**

Have you ever received an unexpected gift that defied the usual boundaries? For me, one particular gift didn't come at Christmas time. When I went to Israel in 2018, I discovered my friend Doreen, a licensed tour guide, had given me a new name: Jenni Swift—"Swiftly," for short.

This thoroughly delighted me! I have asked her so many questions over the years about birds in the Holy Land. When I went in 2015, I discovered that migrating African swifts grace the Western Wall from spring to summer. I *had* to see them, so I centered the timing of my 2018 visit around their migration—hence, my fantastic name change.

Swifts give us a beautiful analogy of God's great love for us, His little flock. The lessons I've learned from these birds help us open the gift of *God's care*.

Once the phenomenon of the swifts sparked my curiosity, I looked up every instance of birds in the Bible. Psalm 84 brought fresh revelation to my mind:

"How lovely is your dwelling place, LORD Almighty! My soul yearns, even faints, for the courts of the LORD; my heart and my flesh cry out for the living God. Even the sparrow has found a home, and the swallow a nest for herself, where she may have her young—a place near your altar, LORD Almighty, my King and my God. Blessed are those who dwell in your house; they are ever praising you" (**Psalm 84:1-5, NIV**).

I realized the place described in this psalm is an actual place. At the Western Wall—the location Jewish people revere as the presence of God and the closest place they can pray to the Temple Mount—relentless chirping emanates. Sparrows, doves, and pigeons—and in certain seasons, swifts—flit around. Little nests are tucked in crevices everywhere.

God's care provides everything our swifts, represented by swallows[40] in Scripture, need. They live as close to the Temple Mount as they can get. They sing for joy to the living God, have their home, and keep their young near His altars. God also sends dedicated humans to help them. Conservation groups exist in Israel ensuring the birds' habitats remain as untouched as possible.

Isn't it amazing that God cares for us even more? I love that something as simple as a bird's nest on an ancient wall can illuminate God's care in our lives.

The words surrounding Jesus' comment about us as His "little flock" tell us how we should receive this care: by avoiding the anxiety we let perch in our souls. Let's apply this truth. Look up the following verses in Luke and write down the primary truth in each.

Luke 12:22

_____

_____

_____

Luke 12:28

_____

_____

_____

Luke 12:31

_____

_____

_____

Luke 12:33

_____

_____

_____

Luke 12:34

_____

_____

_____

As we enjoy the Lord's care today, let's be diligent to imitate the birds: remain in God's presence, sing with joy to the living God, and instruct people around us with His Word. In this way, our waiting-in-heaven nest egg is truly secure.

 PRAYER

Lord, we praise You for Your sovereignty over everything on the earth, and for the examples of Your love for us in nature. We are grateful for the great care You lavish upon us. Help us to open and receive this gift well every single day. In Jesus' name, Amen.

CHRISTMAS QUIETUDE

Meditate on one of today's verses and ask God to remind you of the extravagant care He has shown you. Write down one significant lesson from your quiet time with the Lord.

_____

_____

_____

_____

_____

_____

_____

_____

_____

_____

_____

_____

_____

_____

_____

_____

WORSHIP † *"Carol of the Birds"*

I discovered this sweet Christmas song that showcases birds and their chirping worship. Let's join our feathered friends and tweet, "Noel, Noel!"

Carol of the Birds

When rose the eastern star,

The birds came from a-far,

In that full might of glory.

With one melodious voice

They sweetly did rejoice

And sang the wondrous story.

Sang, praising God on high,

Enthroned above the sky,

And his fair mother Mary.

The eagle left his lair,

Came winging through the air,

His message loud arising.

And to his joyous cry

The sparrow made reply,

His answer sweetly voicing

"O'ercome are death and strife,

This night is born new life",

The robin sang rejoicing.

Ooooh.

When rose the eastern star,

The birds came from a-far.

This is from an overlook into Jerusalem from the Mount of Olives. This is the city lamented over by Jesus from the location where He will return in the future. Knowing He will come again gives us hope. Take heart if you are going through a rough season; it will not last forever.

PHOTO CREDIT: JENNIFER ELWOOD

Receive the Gift of Lamentation

December

13

READ † **Luke 13**

CONTEMPLATE †

"Oh Jerusalem, Jerusalem,
the city that kills the prophets
and stones those who are sent to
it! How often would I have gathered your children together as a
hen gathers her brood under her
wings, and you were not willing!"

—Luke 13:34, ESV

RECEIVE THE GIFT † **Lamentation**

How are you navigating the end of this year? It may seem as though the good times of Christmas surround everyone . . . but how are *you*? If you are having a tough time this year for any reason, I encourage you to find counsel and prayer warriors to cover you. The last thing any of us needs is a pile of suppressed emotions to deal with in January.

Today's gift is lamentation, which gives us an outlet to process difficult events in our lives. I know—it's not very Christmas-y. But acknowledging when the outside cheer doesn't match inner despair is important. It gives us the ability to shine light into the darkness.

In today's passage, we experience the lamentation of Jesus. He aims very pointed words toward the hardhearted in Jerusalem, the city which will soon witness His death.

Imagine being nearby as Jesus uttered these words. He is in a village teaching and healing, and we cannot believe the blessings we witness. Then the crowd parts as a group of Pharisees approach. They tell Jesus to leave because Herod wants to kill Him! We wonder why in the world our ruler, whom we secretly disdain, is after Jesus. In our minds, we have a moment of lamentation to God—*WHY*?

We hear Jesus' response and long to be a fuzzy chick tucked safely under the wing of Jesus. He is such a good man. This seems a safe place to endure the desperation we feel. We no longer have to scream our woes. Our protector is right there, listening to our mournful chirps.

Because Jesus opened the gift of lamentation, we can take heart that crying out our sorrows is a gift we can open. Pouring out the sadness in our hearts is a beautiful, holy way to engage in relationship with the Lord.

Open your favorite Bible and turn to the Psalms, a book of the Bible that gives encouragement and comfort. Consider how much God wants to take you under His wing to comfort you as your lamentation rises in prayer to His ears.

Psalm 34:18

_____

_____

_____

Psalm 46:1

_____

_____

_____

Psalm 145:14

_____

_____

_____

Psalm 102:1-2

_____

_____

_____

 **PRAYER**

Lord, we are grateful for Your acceptance of lamentation. We praise You for hearing our cries. Thank You for the freedom to come to You through faith because of Your Son's sacrifice on the cross. Please help us open and use this gift well. In Jesus' name, Amen!

CHRISTMAS QUIETUDE

Choose one of the verses above. Meditate on the truth and pour out any sorrows you are experiencing to Jesus in the quiet. Write down a remembrance from your quietude below.

_____

_____

_____

_____

_____

_____

_____

WORSHIP † *"Breath of Heaven"*

This song hearkens to the lamentation of Mary as she contemplates possible challenges in her future as Jesus' mother.

This is salt from the Dead Sea. My friend Kristin St. Martin and I experienced this brackish body of water in 2018 on a busy Independence Day. This place to me will forever smell of freshly barbecued chicken. I wonder if any revelers on the shore that day contemplated the true nature of salt as they seasoned their grilled meats.

PHOTO CREDIT: KRISTIN ST. MARTIN

Receive the Gift of Saltiness

December
14

READ † **Luke 14**

CONTEMPLATE †
"Salt is good, but if salt has lost its taste, how shall its saltiness be restored?"

—Luke 14:34, ESV

RECEIVE THE GIFT † **Saltiness**

Have tantalizing aromas been trailing from your kitchen? The tasty morsels we create delight our tastebuds and are a wonderful tradition of this season. We enjoy baking Christmas treats to bless our neighbors. We pack up the yummies in festive boxes and visit the people who live nearby. Our family lives up a hill in the middle of a pasture. It helps to bridge the gap between us and our neighbors when we deliver gifts to be shared around tables.

I believe Jesus appreciated a good meal shared at a table. Throughout this particular Gospel, we encounter Jesus teaching during eight different meals. He lived a nomadic lifestyle and was dependent on others to feed Him. Jesus didn't waste these opportunities but used them mightily.

Our gift today is *saltiness*, a seasoning for food and a necessary nourishment for our bodies. At the time Jesus uttered today's verse, His audience had an intense understanding that salt represented their covenant with the Lord, which initiated when their ancestors left Egypt.

To further open this gift, let's peer into Scripture and examine how this covenant originally tasted:

> *"You shall season all your grain offerings with salt. You shall not let the salt of the covenant with your God be missing from your grain offering; with all your offerings you shall offer salt."*—**Leviticus 2:13, ESV**

Salt, a preservative, symbolized permanence. In antiquity, this represented the binding, unchanging character of a covenant.[41] Historically, these grain offerings, in the form of unleavened bread, sustained the Israelites during the first Passover. This flat, salted bread provided the energy needed to flee Egyptian captivity and cross the parted Red Sea towards the Promised Land of Israel. Imagine the leftover sensation of salt lingering in the mouths of the fleeing Israelites, reminding them of God's presence and promise as they escaped enslavement.

Let's consider how this applies to us today. As believers, we continue to represent the covenant of salt because we are the salt of the earth![42] We are a gift of seasoning, bringing intensified flavor to the world.

To fully open this gift of saltiness, we need to share it with our world, which appears to be improperly seasoned. Believers should be characterized by the taste experience of a particular kind of salt—freshly smoked. The flavor of this salt is unusual and has a particularly exhilarating taste on the tongue. Its flavor lingers uniquely, perhaps because it is more unusual than table salt.

I want to represent this well and I hope you do, too. Let's ask the Lord to use us as good seasoning to others that is uncommon and lingering. Let's be the salt and sprinkle others this season with deliciously flavored words that point to the best spiritual meal ever—Jesus, the Bread of Life.[43]

PRAYER

We praise You, God, for reflecting Yourself in creation, even in something as simple as salt. Thank You for extending Your covenant of salt to us as believers. We pray that we would be intensely savory salt to those around us. Please help us to be constantly pointing to our main spiritual course: Jesus. Amen.

CHRISTMAS QUIETUDE

In the quiet today, reflect on our verse and consider ways you have been salt to others. Is there anyone in your life that needs Jesus-seasoning? Write down the names of anyone needing salty nourishment from you.

_____

_____

_____

_____

_____

_____

_____

_____

_____

_____

_____

_____

_____

WORSHIP † "The Christmas Song"

Let's continue to contemplate the flavors of Christmas as we listen to this song.

I am overjoyed to share this magnificent painting with you. This is "The Return of the Prodigal Son" by Rembrandt. The light in the painting draws me right to the father's compassionate face. Then the harsh gaze of the elder son finds its way to my eyes. Finally, on bended knee we see the younger son, in tattered rags and shoes, throwing himself upon the mercy of his father.

Receive the Gift of Joy

December
15

READ † **Luke 15**

CONTEMPLATE †
"Just so, I tell you, there is
joy before the angels of God
over one sinner who repents."

—Luke 15:10, ESV

RECEIVE THE GIFT † **Joy**

How do you decorate your table for the season of Advent? If you love candles like I do, perhaps an Advent wreath graces your table. When I was a toddler mom, lighting a flame could easily be disastrous, so I skipped this tradition for many years. Now that those days are behind me, I delight in this lovely, meaningful circle of light on my table during Christmas. It's about time to light the pink *joy* candle, our gift today.

The parables in today's reading beautifully display our gift. We will primarily focus our time considering the parable of the prodigal son. We can learn a lot about joy from the characters in this story. Let's put on the shoes of each and walk through this gift, one perspective at a time. We'll start with the swanky new sandals of the younger son:

> *My life is joy-less. The rules, the work on the farm . . . WHEN DO I FINALLY GET TO LIVE? In my latest pout, I approached flush-with-cash Dad and, with casual swagger, asked for my inheritance. What's the worst he could say? No? Maybe I would get something. At*

least a fatted calf to have a party with . . . I couldn't believe my luck— Dad handed me ALL of it! Oh yeah! Time to enjoy all the happiness money could buy.

Before I knew it, I had spent my entire inheritance. My fickle new friends moved on. What now? I looked down and noticed my shoes— completely trashed. I had no money left to replace them. Then a famine began—great. I needed a job and heard that a pig farm needed workers. Pigs are unclean animals, but I was desperate and took what I could get. When the pig slop started to look appetizing, I remembered the aroma of fresh bread passed out to my father's servants. The memory carried me home, hoping for a bite. I was so hungry my stomach had stopped growling. Maybe Dad would let me work on the farm again . . . .

In the haze of too many steps taken in the throes of starvation, I began to recognize my father's fields. From the house in the distance, I saw a figure take off like a shot. It occurred to me that Mom was going to think I smelled so bad! I was so embarrassed at what I'd become. I considered turning around, but I had nowhere else to go. Then I realized, it wasn't my mom coming toward me—it was Dad . . . and he was running.

I soon found myself in my father's embrace. Covered in hugs and kisses, I managed to croak out in tears the words I had practiced all the way home: "Father, I have sinned against heaven and before you. I am no longer worthy to be called your son."[45] My father replaced my shoes and put a ring on my finger. I didn't deserve any of it! Not only did we consume the freshly baked bread I imagined all the way home, we salivated over fresh barbecue. I had behaved deplorably, but my dad celebrated with love and lavish grace. I was shocked by this unexpected gift. My joy was restored.

Let's contrast this with the functional, well-worn shoes of the older brother:

I have NO time for nonsense. I'm the oldest and I work HARD. I follow the rules and strive for perfection. My younger brother, on the other hand . . . ugh, he is sooooo entitled. He asked for his inheritance and Dad gave it to him! Now I have to work even harder because my half of the farm needs more profit!

One day after some time had passed since my irresponsible brother left home, I saw a hasty departure from the house. It almost looked like Dad running . . . but it couldn't be. He would never run. I asked one of the servants to see what the big deal was. When the servant returned with a report, I was DISGUSTED. My baby brother had shamefully come back asking for a job. I'm not having any of this! My dad tried to explain to me that we should be joyful over my brother's return, but nope! The grace my dad showed angered me, and I stormed off into the fields.

Finally, we slip into the stately, clean shoes of the father:

I have two sons. The oldest—well, I worry about him. He's concerned with tasks, and as a result often sacrifices relationships with the people around him. He's gruff with hired help, but he works hard. I suppose he will be all right. Our youngest—well, he caused most of the gray hair on my head. I often shook my head at his half of the farm. It wasn't nearly as productive as his brother's side. But, maybe he will be okay, too.

Then one day my younger son shoved a dagger in my heart when he asked to sell his inheritance. I could not believe the disrespect. But what could I do? We arranged for the sale, and with a heavy heart, I watched him leave.

After some time, one of our servants came with news. He thought my son was at a farm far away in rags, taking slop to pigs. I was incredulous. I missed him so much, and felt hope of his return begin to stir in my heart. What other response could I have to my precious boy?

Soon my hope was realized when I spied him walking toward the house. I threw off tradition and ran down the road, ready to meet his return. In my overwhelming joy, full of forgiveness, I re-clothed him and got the celebration started. Then I realized my other son was going to be MAD. I needed to find him. True to form, there he was sulking in the field. As I approached, his anger was palpable. He watched the party from a distance, most likely feeling left out. He was so hard-hearted. I assured him that the entire farm was his, and then spoke these words: "It was fitting to celebrate and be glad, for this your brother was dead, and is alive; he was lost, and is found."[46] We should have great joy.

Even in the midst of naysaying, may we follow the examples of the younger son and the father, to fully open the gift of joy today.

 **PRAYER**

Lord, we praise You for the joy You experience when we, your prodigal daughters, proclaim salvation! We thank You that You desire to grow in us a happiness that does not waver. Please help us bring You great glory with our insatiable joy! In Jesus' name, Amen.

CHRISTMAS QUIETUDE

In the quiet today, look up 1 Peter 1:8-9. Peter, who lived his own prodigal son moment when he denied Christ, wrote an insightful understanding of joy later in his life. Contemplate this verse and write down any prodigal areas in your life that call for glorious joy.

_____

_____

_____

_____

_____

_____

_____

_____

_____

_____

WORSHIP † *"Joy To The World"*

Today we will shout out our Joy to the World for our coming Savior during worship.

Joy to the World

Joy to the world

Joy to the world

Joy to the world, the Lord is come

Let earth receive her King

Let every heart prepare Him room

And Heaven and nature sing

And Heaven and nature sing

And Heaven, and Heaven, and nature sing

Joy to the world

Joy to the world

Joy to the World, the Savior reigns!

Let men their songs employ

While fields and floods, rocks, hills and plains

Repeat the sounding joy

Repeat the sounding joy

Repeat, repeat, the sounding joy

Joy to the world, now we sing

Let the earth receive her king

Joy to the world, now we sing

Let the angel voices ring

Joy to the world, now we sing

Let men their songs employ

Joy to the world, now we sing

Repeat the sounding joy

Oh oh

He rules the world with truth and grace

And makes the nations prove

The light of His righteousness

And wonders of His love

And wonders of His love

And wonders of His love

And wonders, wonders, of His love

And wonders, wonders, of His love

Joy to the world, now we sing

Let the earth receive her king

Joy to the world, now we sing

Let the angel voices ring

Here we are, the Weber clan: Jenni, Jeremy, Danae, and Peter. I can't even with our clothes . . . Here is one of the many trees we had the pleasure to decorate together as a family. I hope you experience a little nostalgia as you remember precious days of Christmas past.

Receive the Gift of the Law's Fulfillment

December

16

READ † **Luke 16**

CONTEMPLATE †

"The Law and the Prophets were until John; since then the good news of the kingdom of God is preached, and everyone forces his way into it. But it is easier for heaven and earth to pass away than for one dot of the Law to become void."

—Luke 16:16-17, ESV

RECEIVE THE GIFT † **The Law's Fulfillment**

Does your family decorate a Christmas tree each year? I adore this tradition. As a child, my dad selected a real tree for purchase in early December. He took great care to trim the trunk, secure the aromatic timber in the stand, and ensure proper watering. Then, the lights came out. All four of us kids fussed at the lengthy process involved in placing the tiny illuminations just right. Boxes of decorations waiting on the floor mocked our impatience. Once the light adornment was completed we rushed the tree, ensuring a prominent view for our favorite ornaments.

As we consider the importance of light in our celebrations, let's shine a spotlight on our gift today, *the law's fulfillment.*

Let's begin with a definition of the law. In the original Greek, the word is *nomos*. These are the ceremonial and moral rules, the backbone of Judaism as stated in the Old Testament.[47] In our focus verse today, Jesus included the writings of biblical prophets.

I'll share with you how I felt about the law when I was a new believer. I didn't want to read Leviticus, Numbers, or Deuteronomy. I didn't love the idea of following rigid rules that didn't make sense to me. Relegating the law into the category of "too complicated" was easy to do. However, the law exists in God's Word, and will never disappear. The law begs our attention. It is a mistake to ignore or misunderstand it. The Lord gave us the law to guide us to live our best lives in the way God designed.

The writer's perception of the law in Psalm 119, an acrostic poem giving joyous tribute to the role of the law in our lives, gives us an excellent way to understand it. He demonstrated the light of the law when he wrote, "Your word is a lamp to my feet and a light to my path."[48]

According to this beautiful Scripture, when we understand and keep the law we can receive counsel,[49] not be put to shame,[50] guard purity,[51] turn our eyes from worthless things,[52] be wiser than our enemies,[53] and be kept from evil ways.[54] The law is not something to be scared of because it shows us the illuminated path of God's ways. As we delight in the law, we are more likely to hate the false, dark way of sin.

Before Jesus, the atonement of sin according to the law involved blood sacrifices, specifically the blood of a "perfect" lamb to cover sin. The gift today, the fulfillment of the law, enables us to live covered once and for all by the blood of the final sacrifice of the perfect lamb.[55]

Paul, a later apostle of Jesus, understood this. In his letter to the Galatians, he stated, "But if you are led by the Spirit, you are not under the law."[56] Because of Jesus' final sacrifice, God sent us the Holy Spirit, through belief, who lives in us and guides us.[57] Let's not forget, the law was written by God in tandem with Jesus and the Holy Spirit, who were right there with Him.[58] To be led in the Spirit is to be led in the fulfilled, no-more-sacrifice-needed law. Paul further states, "For the whole law is fulfilled in one word: 'You shall love your neighbor as yourself.'"[59] When we shine the light of the world and steadfast love of Jesus on others, this gift is properly opened.

PRAYER

Lord, we are grateful for Your light-filled, steadfast love. Thank You for sacrificing so much. We are humbly on our knees before You in gratitude for the law and the final, beautiful fulfillment of Jesus. Please help us to fully embrace the law's fulfillment and the light of the world, Jesus, in a way that shines His light to others. Amen!

CHRISTMAS QUIETUDE

In the quiet today, meditate on Galatians 5:14. Is there someone who needs the light of Jesus, the fulfillment, in their lives today? Write down the Lord's message to you in the space below.

_____

_____

_____

_____

_____

_____

_____

_____

_____

WORSHIP † *"Light of Christmas"*

Worship with this wonderful reminder of who Christmas is all about.

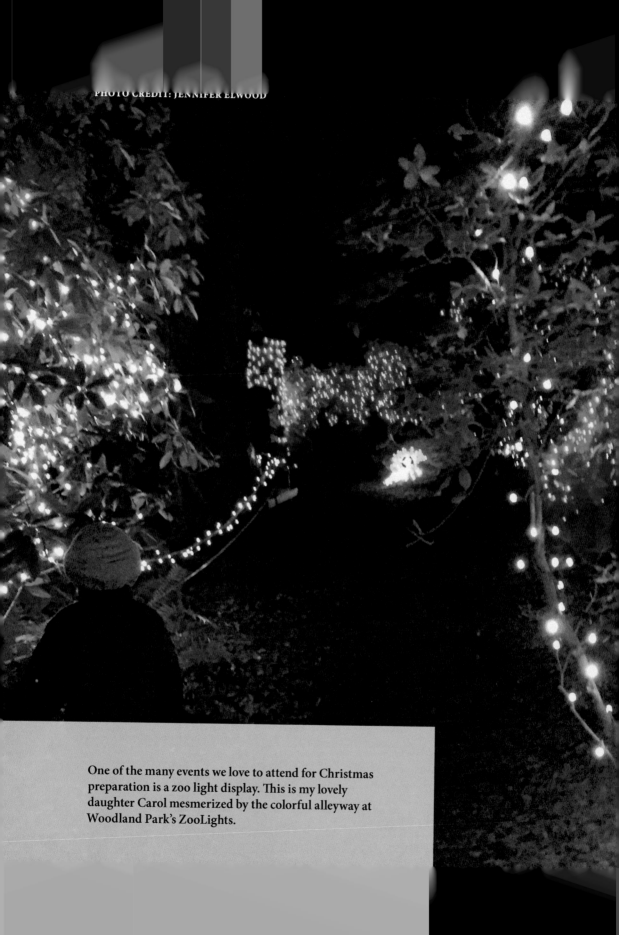

One of the many events we love to attend for Christmas preparation is a zoo light display. This is my lovely daughter Carol mesmerized by the colorful alleyway at Woodland Park's ZooLights.

Receive the Gift of Preparation

December 17

READ † **Luke 17**

CONTEMPLATE †
"Being asked by the Pharisees when the kingdom of God would come, he answered them, 'The kingdom of God is not coming in ways that can be observed, nor will they say, 'Look, here it is!' or 'There!' for behold, the kingdom of God is in the midst of you.'"

—Luke 17:20-21, ESV

RECEIVE THE GIFT † **Preparation**

It's time to ask, "Are you ready for Christmas?" I long to say yes. But who am I kidding? I am rarely ready until past my bedtime on Christmas Eve. The extra time going to kids' concerts, Christmas parties, and preparing special meals takes its toll on a mama's schedule.

Here is a much better question to ask: "Is your heart prepared for Christmas?" Answering this question can help you receive today's gift, *preparation*. My fervent hope for this year is an emotionally and spiritually fulfilling Christmas because we have prepared well. In my opinion, preparing well includes daily washing our minds in the truth of Scripture.

Let's survey the New Testament to process biblical truths regarding how God has and is preparing us for tasks He designed to bring Him glory. If we prepare our hearts with these truths, the exhaustion of last-minute to-do items need not be daunting.

Take your favorite Bible, write down the following verses, and consider God's role in our preparation. Let's create room for peace, not panic, in our hearts as we prepare for Christmas.

God prepares us for action.

1 Peter 1:13

_____

_____

_____

God's workmanship prepares us to glorify Him.

Ephesians 2:10

_____

_____

_____

God prepares us with spiritual tools.

Ephesians 6:14-15

_____

_____

_____

God prepares refreshment in the presence of adversity.

Psalm 23:5

_____

_____

_____

God prepares us for Jesus' return.

John 14:3

_____

_____

_____

PRAYER

We praise You, Lord, for the many ways You prepare us for the future. We thank You for Your intricate plans to prepare good things for us. Please help us slow down and ready ourselves for the establishment of Your plan in this season. In Jesus' name, Amen.

CHRISTMAS QUIETUDE

In the quiet today, choose one verse above for meditation. Write down any needed steps of preparation to obtain peace this Christmas.

_____

_____

_____

_____

_____

_____

WORSHIP † *"O Come, O Come Emmanuel"*

I love this wonderful song that prepares our hearts so well for Christmas. If you are able to access the playlist on the website or social media, the link will take you to a version of this song performed in English and Hebrew. Bonus: It was filmed in Israel.

Did you know that the *shekel* is the currency in Israel?
Here are examples of modern-day 1/10, 1/2 and 1 Shekel.
May we, inspired by the humility of the tax-collector, be
reminded to use money this season in a God-honoring way.

Receive the Gift of Humility

December
18

READ † **Luke 18**

CONTEMPLATE †
"But the tax collector, standing far off, would not even lift up his eyes to heaven, but beat his breast, saying, 'God, be merciful to me, a sinner!'"

—Luke 18:13, ESV

RECEIVE THE GIFT † **Humility**

Have you been to any Christmas music concerts this year? As you can tell, I *love* Christmas music. Attending live music events delights me. This season also marks special worship music at church. I play keys periodically with my church's worship band. Each time I receive a request, I have my work cut out for me. I don't glance at the music. I attempt to prepare well and engage in worship even before I step foot into a rehearsal.

It would be easy while on the platform in the Worship Center to "perform" every Sunday. Raising ourselves on a platform tempts us to engage in pride. Instead, posturing ourselves to give God glory helps us open the gift of *humility*.

I adore the direction given to open humility from our Scripture passage today. We have instruction straight from the lips of Jesus: we are to approach Him as a child. Can you imagine being in the crowd with your precious baby, hoping Jesus will linger and glance at or touch your little one? The image of Jesus blessing children in the crowd is beautiful.

The disciples' response gives us a different angle to view the gift as they receive a dose of humility from Jesus. Perhaps their response to Him came from a pompous place. They've relegated Jesus' attention to what is "important" in their minds. Further instruction demonstrated how freely Jesus' touch is available to all of us.

By extension, with child-like innocence, we can skip up to the throne and throw our arms around God the Father. This is a precious gift available to us through belief in Jesus, and is something God longs for us to open.

Perhaps you're wondering, "Can I *really* demonstrate humility?" In a world where me, myself, and I are of great importance, the thought appears daunting. Our brick-hard heads and hearts challenge us at times. Tucked in this chapter of the Bible is the not-so-secret way to realize this gift. "What is impossible with man is possible with God."[60]

We cannot open humility by ourselves. Only by Christ's grace and power can this happen. We encountered a wonderful example of humility in the tax collector in our focus verse. Let's take another walk through Scripture and examine what else we can accomplish while holding God's hand in our search for genuine humility. The peace that results is necessary as the hectic Christmas season reaches its fevered pitch. Let these attributes wash over you as we prepare for the count up through the last week to Christmas.

PATIENCE

"Be completely humble and gentle; be patient, bearing with one another in love."—**Ephesians 4:2, NIV**

VALUING OTHERS

"Do nothing out of selfish ambition or vain conceit. Rather, in humility value others above yourselves."—**Philippians 2:3, NIV**

WISDOM

"When pride comes, then comes disgrace, but with humility comes wisdom."—**Proverbs 11:2, NIV**

THE BEST CLOTHING EVER

"Therefore, as God's chosen people, holy and dearly loved, clothe yourselves with compassion, kindness, humility, gentleness and patience."—**Colossians 3:12, NIV**

GRACE

"In the same way, you who are younger, submit yourselves to your elders. All of you, clothe yourself with humility toward one another, because, 'God resists the proud but shows favor to the humble.'"—**1 Peter 5:5-6, NIV**

PROPER AWE AND REVERENCE TO THE LORD

"Humility is the fear of the LORD; its wages are riches and honor and life."—**Proverbs 22:4, NIV**

FORGIVENESS

"If my people, who are called by my name, will humble themselves and pray and seek my face and turn from their wicked ways, then I will hear from heaven, and I will forgive their sin and will heal their land."—**2 Chronicles 7:14, NIV**

HONOR

"Pride brings a person low, but the lowly in spirit gain honor."—**Proverbs 29:23, NIV**

God is willing and able to do the impossible in your life. Open this gift, humble yourself, and observe how the Lord uses your obedience to bring peace.

 PRAYER

Lord, we are so grateful that childlike faith is the standard in Your Kingdom. Thank You for displaying Your power through us as we open the gift of humility. Please help us remain in pursuit of selflessness throughout our lives. In Your humble Son's name, Amen.

CHRISTMAS QUIETUDE

Choose a verse from the above list. Meditate in the quiet. Write down how the Lord desires to further humble your heart as we enter the final count up to Christmas.

_____

_____

_____

_____

_____

_____

_____

_____

_____

_____

_____

_____

WORSHIP † *"Fullness of Grace"*

Keith and Kristyn Getty's Christmas album is a collection of music worth savoring. Worship with this beautiful song about how Jesus humbly entered our world.

Fullness of Grace

Fullness of Grace in man's human frailty,

This is the wonder of Jesus.

Laying aside His power and glory,

Humbly He entered our world.

Chose the path of meanest worth:

Scandal of a virgin birth.

Born in a stable, cold and rejected:

Here lies the hope of the world.

Fullness of grace, the love of the Father

Shown in the face of Jesus.

Stooping to bear the weight of humanity,

Walking the Calvary road.

Christ the holy Innocent

Took our sin and punishment.

My wonderful artist friend Cindy created this watercolor painting of Zacchaeus just for us. A 2,000-year-old Sycamore Fig tree exists in Jericho and is by tradition the tree. She started by re-creating the tree of today and added the rest as she imagined what Israel was like in the 1st century. This painting transports me to that moment as he waited for Jesus. I hope this lovely image does the same for you.

cindy Trudd

Receive the Gift of Transformation

December

19

READ † **Luke 19**

CONTEMPLATE †
"For the Son of Man came to
seek and save the lost."

—Luke 19:10, ESV

RECEIVE THE GIFT † **Transformation**

Are you enjoying the metamorphosis of decoration around your city? Yard leaves raked and trees barren, perhaps there is a covering of snow blanketing the ground. Magical, twinkling lights shine everywhere. My family enjoys weaving up and down side streets in the evening when we have the time to look at light displays. We yell, "CHRISTMAS LIGHTS!" and call out which side of the car to look. We also keep a tally of the number of homes that display a lit-up baby Jesus somewhere in their outdoor decor.

I'm so glad other people are able to tidy up sufficiently to showcase their beautiful display of lights. By this time of year, our American Sycamore tree hasn't dropped half its leaves and the messy seed pods annoy us constantly. I wish the wintertime change would speed up so our garden clean up would near completion, but that is impossible. It will take patience to witness the full *transformation*, the gift we are opening today.

Speaking of sycamores—the less annoying fig variety, that is—let's walk together through this portion of Scripture. Our friend and fellow believer, Zacchaeus, helps us open the gift of transformation by climbing one of these trees.

My name, Zacchaeus, means pure.[61] The expectation to live an unblemished life began early. My parents expected me to morally stand tall— but how could I, short and poor as I was? As a child, people made fun of my size, and I hated it. Someday, I would make them pay—literally.

I went with my parents to "pay Caesar" one day and noticed the tax collector's nice clothing. He obviously earned (or stole) a lot of money. I wanted lots of money someday. Sure, the tax collectors demanded a little extra, but they needed to look good for their job. Everyone hated them, but I didn't care. When I grew up, I wanted this kind of life—the kind that didn't want for anything and required respect from everyone.

My parents were frustrated when I got my first job. They didn't understand my needs. It didn't take long to have extra money and start living the good life. People were afraid of me because I possessed the real power of having a job in the Roman government. I could take extra from anyone, and no one would say anything. It didn't take long to have a nice wardrobe and eat rich food every day.

One day, I received a promotion to chief tax collector! I was sent to Jericho, the City of Palms, and couldn't believe my luck—those tall trees all over reminded me of how high up I finally was. Lucky me, this place is flush with cash. It is the only place in the world growing balsam, used to make the medicine and perfume that everyone wants.[62] It's also on the trade route that goes everywhere.[63] The economy was booming and I got super rich, taking a cut from every single person who worked for me. I kept telling myself I deserved it, but something was starting to bother me.

Occasionally, I would think back to my education of the Scriptures and remember a psalm of David. He asked the questions, "Who shall ascend the hill of the LORD? And who shall stand in his holy place?"[64] The answer he gives is, "He who has clean hands and a pure heart, who does not lift up his soul to what is false and does not swear deceitfully."[65] That is not me. I'm rich now and no one makes fun of my height anymore, but I'm not standing tall. Clean hands and a pure heart, like my name, are something I've polluted with evil actions. Is there anyone who can help me stop this corrupt life?

I heard rumors about a man named Jesus up in the north on the Sea of Galilee, who was performing miracles and healing everyone. People said he was from Nazareth, but it must have been a mistake, because everyone knows nothing good comes from there. I heard he was headed this way and decided I had to see him. A huge crowd surrounded him, and no one would let me get close. With my heart and mind racing, I bounded up the route through town and found a nice, big Sycamore Fig tree to climb. I sat on a limb that felt like it was created just for me, and waited in the shade of the leaves.

I saw the crowd getting closer and felt lucky to have a bird's-eye view of the event. Suddenly, Jesus saw me and approached me. Somehow, he knew my name—and invited himself to come to my house! I hurried down and led him on the way. The Pharisees grumbled, but I didn't care. I burst in the door and ordered a magnificent feast to be prepared. My house filled up for the first time in ages with all sorts of people. As time went on and I heard Jesus speak, the weight of every penny I ever extracted from my fellow man weighed me down.

I'd heard that this remarkable man preached, "Blessed are the pure in heart, for they shall see God." [66] I had no doubt that God was in my house, but where was my pure heart? I decided to believe, and I was transformed. I no longer desired blessing from people. I wanted the blessing of God. It was time to turn from sin and the weight of all the money I stole.

I turned my gaze to Jesus and blurted out, "Behold, Lord, the half of my goods I give to the poor. And if I have defrauded anyone of anything, I restore it fourfold." [67] A gasp rippled through the crowd. Somehow they knew I wasn't paying lip service but really meant what I said. I would lose my wealth, but I didn't care about that anymore. Jesus, not surprised, looked right in my eyes and told me, "Today, salvation has come to this house." [68] Sweet relief swept over me. He then said, "For the Son of Man came to seek and to save the lost." [69] So very lost in my sin, I couldn't believe my luck—well, not luck ... blessing. Jesus sought short, little me in the tree and sent me higher—forgiven and saved. Now that my transformation is complete, it's time to bring out my stockpile of money and begin the journey to set things right. It's time to fully receive blessing from the LORD and righteousness from the God of my salvation! [70]

PRAYER

Lord, we praise You for Your transformational power! Thank You for this gift that, by your grace, we can experience. Please help us to be faithful in sharing the change You have brought about in our lives. We desire so very much to glorify You. Amen!

CHRISTMAS QUIETUDE

In today's quiet, meditate on our verse and consider what God desires to transform in you. Write down something God is stirring to change.

_____

_____

_____

_____

_____

_____

_____

_____

_____

_____

_____

WORSHIP † *"Away in a Manger"*

Let's look down, perched with Zacchaeus in the Sycamore, upon Jesus as we worship today.

Away in a Manger

Away in a manger

No crib for His bed

The little Lord Jesus

Lay down His sweet head

The stars in the sky

Look down where He lay

The little Lord Jesus

Asleep on the hay

The cattle are lowing

The poor Baby wakes

But little Lord Jesus

No crying He makes

I love Thee, Lord Jesus

Look down from the sky

And stay by my side

'Til morning is nigh

Be near me, Lord Jesus

I ask Thee to stay

Close by me forever

And love me, I pray

Bless all the dear children

In Thy tender care

And take us to Heaven

To live with Thee there

Jesus, our cornerstone. Perhaps as you consider making future gingerbread houses, a new tradition could include Jesus in your creation as a reminder of who He is.

Receive the Gift of the Cornerstone

December 20

CONTEMPLATE †

"Jesus looked directly at them and asked, 'Then what is the meaning of that which is written:

'The stone the builders rejected has become the cornerstone?'"

—Luke 20:17, NIV

RECEIVE THE GIFT † The Cornerstone

Do you craft a gingerbread house during your Christmas festivities? This is a beloved tradition for our family. Perhaps like me, through many cookie-house building adventures, you discovered not all gingerbread houses are equal. Over the years, we tried different types—pre-assembled, big ones, small ones . . . I am personally a fan of the pre-assembled. Who has the patience to wait for the icing to solidify? If you don't wait long enough, you end up with a MESS! We experienced, more than once, a hurricane of broken cookies, sloppy frosting, and candies piled on a plate. Through these experiences, I've learned the key to a stable house is a well-prepared foundation.

The thought of crumbling foundations causes gratitude for our gift today, *the cornerstone*. This attribute of Jesus demands our attention. A cornerstone is an object of high importance, which something else depends upon.[71] Jesus, who represents our gift from today fully opened, is a rock not cut by human hands, upon whom we can build our faith.[72] He is our unfailing, firm foundation.[73]

To open the gift of Jesus' cornerstone declaration (originally from Psalm 118:22), it is important for us to understand the parable of the vineyard. Let me take your hand and whisk you away, like the Dickensian ghost of Christmas past, to a vantage point hovering above a dirt field ready to receive the planting of grapevines.

Imagine the pastoral scene. Soil, worked and prepared, awaits the planting of a vineyard during a warm spring season. The owner built a wall around the new creation with a lookout tower for protection. Anticipating future fruit production, he constructed wine presses in the ground.[74]

In the first year, the shoots must establish a well-anchored root system, so the workers provided supports for the developing shoots. The owner left responsibility for this land to the tenant farmers. He trusted their continued work to ensure the vines developed properly for the next three years.

Growing vineyards was not a speedy process; waiting for proper growth required patience. In the second year, workers severely pruned the plants. Soil nutrients and drainage needed to be carefully checked. The employees worked diligently but remained unable to harvest.

Then finally in the third year, if weather, soil, pruning, and ripening all work in perfect harmony, the grape harvest occurred.

Over time, the hearts of the workers hardened. They decided they would not give up any fruits from their labor. Wine production commenced and monetary profit became reality. However, the owner, after three years away, sent messengers in waves to receive his share. The emissaries returned to him with tales of abuse. Perplexed, the owner sent his son, expecting success. But the evil workers killed him. With delusions of grandeur, they still expected full profit from their work. The grieving father returned in wrath. He ended the lives of those who killed his son and passed the inheritance to others.[75]

The murder of the vineyard owner's son reminds us of the death of our Savior, doesn't it? Jesus experienced the brutal necessity of rejection and laid down His life in order to take His place as the cornerstone and mediator of the Church. We all have a choice—to reject God's gift or embrace it. When our branches are anchored on the real vine of our Father, we have increased security on the cornerstone.[76] When we accept the gift and place Jesus as our cornerstone, the foundation for our lives remains secure.

PRAYER

Lord, from the vines of the field to the rocks under our feet, we praise You for the gift of Your Son, our Cornerstone. Please help us to stand firm on Christ and have confidence in the rock You gave us to stand on! Help us to be living stones with infinite trust in the solid base, Your Son. In Jesus' name, Amen.

CHRISTMAS QUIETUDE

In the quiet, meditate on John 15:5. Ask God to reveal any tendrils of sin that are wrapped around your heart and mind and how He desires to untangle you from them. Write down any steps that come to mind.

_____

_____

_____

_____

_____

_____

_____

_____

_____

WORSHIP † *"The Holly and the Ivy"*

This Christmas song illuminates nature as a reminder of Christ and helps us contemplate the birth of our Cornerstone.

Here's my family with Santa Corky. Imagine this photo, but in our future home with God on the throne. It will be heavenly.

Receive the Gift of Our Future Home

READ † **Luke 21**

CONTEMPLATE †
"Now when these things begin to happen, straighten up and raise your heads, because your redemption is drawing near."
—Luke 21:28, ESV

RECEIVE THE GIFT † **Our Future Home**

I have a somewhat controversial question for you: Do you celebrate Christmas with Santa? I polled this topic on social media and received a wide variety of answers. Santa seems to be a source of wonder and magic, as well as controversy.

As a family, we highly anticipate Santa's visit to our Christmas party each year. When my friend Tracey married "Santa Corky," our Christmas party tradition transformed. Watching with wonder at the collective reaction from children and adults alike, Santa Corky appeared in the entryway with a bellowing "Ho! Ho! Ho!" and swept into the chair of honor in the living room. Santa's "meter" came out, and the children pealed with cheers as they received the rating of "nice." Then, Santa read an account of Jesus' birth from Scripture and told the kids about how much he loves Jesus. Family pictures and gift requests began, and the love was felt even after the party ended. The wonderful memories continue to last years later.

Though I enjoy many aspects of my life on earth, uncertainty of the future feels unnerving. Santa's presence at Christmastime, while lovely, fails to remove anxiety. The lack of peace causes me look forward to *our future home*, the gift we are opening today.

In a way, our future home doesn't seem like a gift. When it comes, the one we live in now will no longer exist. Jesus informs us of this as He builds on yesterday's distressing news of Jerusalem's impending destruction (which occurred in 70 AD) with more ruin that will take place before He creates the new heaven and earth. The birth pains will be devastating for a time. As I write this, my county is on month four of Coronavirus lockdown, so I'm feeling "these things" intensely. But all of this *must* happen to prepare us for the glory of God to come in the home of our forever church. Knowing this gives us preparatory information and provides hope.

The instruction given to Daniel after the prophesy he received is a perfect way to frame this reality. "And you? Go about your business without fretting or worrying. Relax. When it's all over, you will be on your feet to receive your reward."[77]

Though unnerving, future events as told through Scripture mean to inform us. Instruction like this is critical. As Jesus says later in Luke 21:36, "Keep alert at all times. And pray that you might be strong enough to escape these coming horrors and stand before the Son of Man."[78] The strength to escape will come for the Lord Himself. This news should not be received as distressing, but informative. As believers, we can trust that He will care for us no matter what.

So, what is the best action we can take in light of the future? Our eyes must shift to a focus beyond the horizon of difficult times. As Jesus' return becomes imminent, we view the rise of heaven.

Intense, focused vision on our future home helps us endure anything. For me, the image of heaven evokes thoughts of peace and an intimacy with God never experienced before. No more tears, death, pain, or sorrow.[79] We'll receive a new body more like Jesus' glorious body.[80] We'll enjoy a wonderful feast, prepared by the Lord Himself.[81] Very best of all, uninterrupted worship of the Lord occurs day and night: "Holy, Holy, Holy, is the Lord God Almighty, who was and is and is to come!"[82]

These truths prompt me to ask one more controversial, but necessary, question: Do you believe that Jesus is God's Son, sent to save us? If the answer is "no" or "I'm not sure," let's chat. Please get in touch with me or speak to someone in your life who you know has the kind of hope in the Lord that I am speaking of here. If you are ready, or have already believed, pray the following prayer.

PRAYER

Lord, I am so thankful that You are sovereign over everything! I understand my sin separates me from God's presence. I believe in Your Son Jesus, who died for my sins on the cross. I put my faith in You. Please help me to believe! I want to experience everlasting life in Your presence. In Your Son's Holy name, Amen.

CHRISTMAS QUIETUDE

In the quiet, meditate on the truth of your future home. Allow thoughts of the resurrected Jesus in heaven with the Father to wash over you. Write down a note of gratitude to Jesus for your salvation.

_____

_____

_____

_____

_____

_____

_____

_____

WORSHIP † *"He Shall Reign Forevermore"*

Let's worship the Lord, our forever King!

This is my first communion experience at the Garden Tomb in Jerusalem. The darkened doorway in the distance beyond the bread and cup is a first-century tomb discovered on the northern outskirts of Jerusalem in 1885.

Receive the Gift of Communion

December
22

READ † **Luke 22**

CONTEMPLATE †
"And he took bread, and when he
had given thanks, he broke it and
gave it to them, saying, 'This is
my body, which is given for you.
Do this in remembrance of me.'"

—Luke 22:19, ESV

RECEIVE THE GIFT † **Communion**

Are there any traditions you're still thinking about squeezing in this year?
At around this time, if I've not already brought him out, the Elf on the Shelf
is in the realm of consideration. I own a cute vintage one that came from
an estate sale. Sprinkles, the jingle-jolly elf who loves Jesus, shows up and
delights my girls (when I remember). We find him in precarious situations
with written suggestions of grace-filled actions toward others. He prompts
us to bake gifts for neighbors and take kindness breaks with each other
throughout the day. This helps punctuate the season for my girlies, and my
older son enjoys "helping" Sprinkles into the next position when everyone
else is in bed.

We find an even better tradition to enhance our Christmas celebrations as we open our gift for today, *communion*. With just a few days until

we celebrate Christ's birth, a remembrance of Jesus' sacrifice on the cross may be what we need to truly celebrate our Savior.

Let's set the scene in the upper room where this event took place. According to the accounts in Matthew 26, Mark 14, and Luke 22, Jesus' last supper occurred at the beginning of the Festival of Unleavened Bread. The Jewish people begin festivals the night preceding, which is when the Passover feast occurred.

The Haggadah, today's procedure for the Passover meal, developed over time after the destruction of Jerusalem in 70 AD. Jewish people, forced from their homeland, then had a significant way to remember this appointed festival. In Jesus' time, it is not certain how much of this tradition existed.[83] However, Moses offered God's instruction for this festival to the Israelites in Exodus 13:3-10 as their flight from Egypt began. God repeated this instruction to remember this event with unleavened foods multiple times across the books of Exodus, Leviticus, Numbers, and Deuteronomy.

Jesus and His disciples clearly followed the instruction to remember the Passover. The Festival of Unleavened Bread required seven days of eating no yeast to help participants remember the haste in food preparation required to flee from Egypt. Lack of yeast historically signified the absence of sin, which made this particular bread a perfect representation of Jesus.

With foreshadowing heartbreak, Jesus broke the bread and announced its representation of His body, broken for us. He follows with the cup, representing His soon-to-be shed blood.

The next day, the sacrifice of the Passover lamb would take place in the Temple. The first time this event happened, the enslaved Israelites used the blood of the lamb to paint their doorposts so the angel of death would "pass over" their homes and not kill their firstborn. Each subsequent year, this sacrifice and remembrance was repeated. The New Covenant meant Jesus would be the final sacrifice needed to cover sins. In fact, the following day would witness the sacrifice of the lamb *and* the Lamb.

Jesus not only fulfilled the final sacrifice, He left a new remembrance for the Church that would come. Paul, in 1 Corinthians 11:17-34, corrected wrong practices regarding communion. He repeated instruction from the Gospel accounts in verses 23-26:

> *"For I received from the Lord what I also delivered to you, that the Lord Jesus on the night when he was betrayed took bread, and when he had given thanks, he broke it, and said, 'This is my body, which is for you. Do this in remembrance of me.' In the same way also he took the cup, after supper, saying, 'This cup is the new covenant in my blood. Do this, as often as you drink it, in remembrance of me.' For as often as you eat this bread and drink the cup, you proclaim the Lord's death until he comes."*[84]

Paul also pointed out the need for self-examination. Judgement rests on those who abuse this holy commemoration.[85]

Let's do as Jesus commands and, with fellow believers, embrace gratitude while we remember His sacrifice through communion. Without it, we have no real reason to celebrate Christmas.

PRAYER

Lord, thank You for the gift of communion. We are so grateful that You sent Your Son so we could be in relationship with You. We praise You for this sign of remembrance, which helps unify Your church. We proclaim the name of Your precious Son, Amen.

CHRISTMAS QUIETUDE

In the quiet today, consider the New Covenant and everything Jesus did to bring it to pass. Meditate on our verse and engage in a time of confession. If you are able sometime today, participate in communion with a fellow believer.

_____

_____

_____

_____

_____

_____

_____

_____

_____

_____

_____

_____

_____

_____

WORSHIP † *"Silent Night"*

Let's consider these hours of darkness. Painful prayer, betrayal, arrest, beating, and the cross awaited Jesus the very next day. Imagine the walk, perhaps in silence, to the Garden of Gethsemane that evening. With this in mind, consider parallels to the silent night we will celebrate in three days.

Silent Night

Silent night, holy night
All is calm, all is bright
'Round yon virgin Mother and Child
Holy infant so tender and mild
Sleep in heavenly peace
Sleep in heavenly peace

Silent night, holy night!
Shepherds quake at the sight!
Glories stream from heaven afar;
Heavenly hosts sing Al-le-lu-ia!

Christ the Savior is born!
Christ the Savior is born!
Christ the Savior is born!

Silent night, holy night
Son of God, oh, love's pure light
Radiant beams from Thy holy face
With the dawn of redeeming grace
Jesus, Lord at Thy birth
Jesus, Lord at Thy birth
Jesus, Lord at Thy birth

This site in Israel, Dominus Flevit, rests next to the Garden of Gethsemane at the base of the Mount of Olives. This less tended garden contains olive trees and, in spring, tiny red poppies. The flowers bloom all over Israel right around Passover every year. Jesus shed the first drops of blood for us from His sweat as he prayed in Gethsemane the night before the crucifixion. (Luke 22:44) Don't these look like nature crying out, remembering the night of His reckoning?

Receive the Gift of Jesus' Obedience

December 23

READ † **Luke 23**

CONTEMPLATE †

"Then Jesus, calling out with a loud voice, said, 'Father, into your hands I commit my spirit!' And having said this he breathed his last."

—Luke 23:46, ESV

RECEIVE THE GIFT † **Jesus' Obedience**

Today is the heaviest day in all of Scripture. *Jesus' obedience*, the gift we open on the eve of Christmas Eve, is a wooden cross wrapped in a bow of crimson blood. It would be a disservice to gloss over the crucifixion, even as we wonder at Mary and Joseph's imminent arrival in Bethlehem and the subsequent birth of Jesus. To celebrate the baby Jesus also celebrates the man to come. The Son of Man lived out Good Friday in the most brutally heart-wrenching, loving, God-ordained event experienced by humankind. Though challenging, it is a gift worth opening today.

Let's think back to the lesson from Luke 1 when we opened the gift of prayer. We witnessed the multitude of people at the Temple praying. Fast forward thirty-three years: God fully answered their prayers, and the Savior is here. But most of the people are completely blind to it. Perhaps some of the people who previously marveled at a mute Zechariah are there. But now?

They are not praying. Their prayers weren't answered the way they expected, so their words became bitter accusations. Shouting replaced prayer. Can you imagine the cacophony of angry, bitter men accusing Jesus? Their abusive words soon turn into blows, both physical and emotional.

And then Jesus, opening today's gift for us, sacrificed Himself. The perfect, unblemished lamb died unfairly for every sin ever committed—past, present, and future. We should acknowledge His crucifixion with tears of sorrow and deep gratitude. If He hadn't gone through with the cross, every single sin would send us straight into forever darkness. Jesus' obedience to die gave us life—just for the cost of simple belief in Him. What a gracious gift we have in these words of Scripture today.

As we prepare to kneel before the manger made from a tree to marvel at the birth of Jesus, let's remember this: Our true calling to obedience is to pull two shards from our Savior's first crib and cross them over one another. Let's deny ourselves, pick up our crosses, and follow the example of Jesus' perfect obedience.[86]

PRAYER

Lord Jesus, we praise Your example of true, unwavering obedience to God the Father. Please help us experience joy and peace today in the midst of sorrowful remembrance at the cross. Please illuminate people in our path today who need to know how much they are loved by the Savior of the world, the God-baby who grew into the God-man for this very moment. In the precious name of Your Son, Amen.

CHRISTMAS QUIETUDE

In the quiet, praise God for the gift we receive through Jesus' obedience, eternal life through faith. Write down any steps of obedience the Lord lays on your heart.

_____

_____

_____

_____

_____

_____

_____

_____

_____

_____

_____

_____

_____

_____

_____

_____

WORSHIP † *"This is War"*

The obedience that led Jesus to the cross enabled Him, with the full authority of the Father, to declare war on death. Let's worship with an unusual Christmas song that is absolutely perfect.

This is a first-century tomb found under the Convent of the Sisters of Nazareth. I was stunned at the amazing site found deep below ground in Jesus' former hometown.

Receive the Gift of Everlasting Life

December
24

READ † **Luke 24**

CONTEMPLATE †

"And as they were frightened and bowed their faces to the ground the men said to them, 'Why do you seek the living among the dead? He is not here, but has risen. Remember how he told you, while he was still in Galilee, that the Son of Man must be delivered into the hands of sinful men and be crucified and on the third day rise.'"

—Luke 24:5-7, ESV

RECEIVE THE GIFT † **Everlasting Life**

He is risen! And Merry Christmas Eve! Did you enjoy reading the joyful account of Jesus' resurrection today? I always do. Too often, we separate the miracle of Jesus' birth from the resurrection of our Savior. The gift we open today, *everlasting life*, helps us frame well the deeper meaning of celebrating Jesus' entry to the world.

Instead of reading a lesson today, set aside extra time for your Christmas Quietude this evening before you go to bed. A few minutes by the light of the tree adorned with wrapped gifts is the perfect time to recollect the gifts you received from the Lord this month. Savor them. Release anything that will prevent you from having a full, focused celebration tomorrow. I encourage you to take some time to make use of the extra journaling space below.

I pray you'll have a Merry Christmas fully saturated with God's perfect peace.

Lord, we are incredibly grateful for Your Son's guidance in our lives. We are very thankful to Him for enabling us to enjoy Your eternal presence. I pray the abundance of gifts we received from Your Word this month will permeate our souls and encourage us to have a peace-centered, joy-filled Christmas. In Your Son's name, Amen.

CHRISTMAS QUIETUDE

_____

_____

_____

_____

_____

_____

_____

_____

_____

_____

_____

_____

_____

_____

_____

_____

_____

_____

_____

_____

_____

_____

_____

_____

_____

_____

_____

_____

_____

WORSHIP † *"Oh Holy Night"*

A song for worship by the light of the tree this evening.

A candle on the floor at the Church of the Beatitudes.
Such a peaceful sight for Christmas Day.

Receive the Bonus Gift of Peace

December 25

† Christmas Day

RECEIVE THE GIFT † **Peace**

We made it! Merry Christmas! I truly hope the illumination of Scripture each day this month brought you to a place of settled Christmas *peace*, our final gift from Scripture. I encourage you to engage in one last Christmas Quietude using the Scriptures provided below. Set aside some time today and allow the peace of the Lord to flow over you all.

CONTEMPLATE †

"May the LORD give strength to his people! May the LORD bless his people with peace."—**Psalm 29:11, ESV**

"Great peace have those who love your law, nothing can make them stumble."—**Psalm 119:165, ESV**

"For to us a child is born, to us a son is given; and the government shall be upon his shoulder, and his name shall be called Wonderful, Counselor, Mighty God, Everlasting Father, Prince of Peace."—**Isaiah 9:6, ESV**

"You keep him in perfect peace whose mind is stayed on you, because he trusts in you."—**Isaiah 26:3, ESV**

"O LORD, you will ordain peace for us, for you have indeed done for us all our works."—**Isaiah 26:12, ESV**

"For you shall go out in joy and be led forth in peace; the mountains and hills before you shall break forth into singing, and all the trees of the field shall clap their hands."—**Isaiah 55:12, ESV**

"Peace I leave with you; my peace I give to you. Not as the world gives do I give to you. Let not your hearts be troubled, neither let them be afraid."—**John 14:27, ESV**

"I have said these things to you, that in me you may have peace. In the world you will have tribulation. But take heart; I have overcome the world."—**John 16:33, ESV**

"May the God of hope fill you with all joy and peace in believing, so that by the power of the Holy Spirit you may abound in hope."—**Romans 15:13, ESV**

"Let the peace of Christ rule in your hearts, to which indeed you were called in one body. And be thankful."—**Colossians 3:15, ESV**

"Strive for peace with everyone, and for the holiness without which no one will see the Lord."—**Hebrews 12:14, ESV**

 **PRAYER**

Lord, we praise You for the gift of our Prince of Peace, Jesus. Thank You for sending Your Son to us. We pray for peace over Christmas day. Please help us to rest and delight in the gifts we received from You this month. In Your Son's name, Amen.

WORSHIP † For today's worship, I created a playlist of our worship songs this month and a few extra favorites to enjoy. You can access it on Spotify. The playlist is called "Counting up to Christmas in the Gospel of Luke."

May Jesus bestow many blessed memories upon your day.

Acknowledgements

I imagined writing this section of the book as a child. Never mind the actual work of creating word after word on a page, my naive mind wanted to go straight here. Oh, little Jenni . . . You had no idea how truly sweet opening this gift of gratitude would be.

I have many people to thank who gifted me in countless ways to write my first book.

My first receipt of gratitude goes to God the Father, God the Son, and God the Holy Spirit. From our triune God, we received an inerrant Bible we can depend on to show us great love, give us sound instruction to live by, and exist in forever relationship with us—a great gift to humankind indeed. My writing would be nothing without the love and guidance poured into me from the Lord. In addition, I am crazy thankful for the obedience of Luke and the wonderfully detailed Gospel he released to the world.

Next comes my family. My husband, Tom, read each draft first and provided excellent feedback until it was sent off to the editor. He endured stacks of papers and gave me the gift of feeling valued. Many thanks to my children, Mitchell, Carol, and Ella. I am grateful for the gift of subjects for the book photography as well as the time I received. They heard, "Give me another minute" so many times. Their patience with me exceeded my wildest expectations.

My parents, Jerry and Linda, put up with a lot from me over the years. They gave me the gift of life and ever since gifts of love, encouragement, and support. After they watched me walk through the phase of life I call the "Wild 20s," I think they are praising the Lord that I turned my life toward Him. I am grateful they were there through all of the ups and down. And special thanks to my dad who was literally the feet of Jesus for the photo in Chapter 8.

"A [woman] of noble character who can find? She is worth far more than rubies" (Proverbs 31:10, emphasis mine). To me, this woman is my sister Danae. She is constant and steadfast and I'm overjoyed she shares the jewel of faith in the Lord. She read all the drafts and gifted me with wonderful friendship, loads of love, and excellent guidance. She also gave me the gift of a fun and good-natured niece, Gracie, who supplied art and our depiction of Martha for this book, as well as a sister-style relationship with my children.

A big thank you goes to my fun brothers, Jeremy and Peter Weber. Life is so much more enjoyable with them and their awesome families. I'm thankful that they let me share our family pic.

I need to give a "thanks yo" to my cousin Angie Waddle, who is not only my sister-cousin but gifted this book with her amazing artistic eye to guide which photos and art to include in this book. She birthed the ideas for the Jesus cornerstone gingerbread house and the Bible story reenactment photos. Sheer genius.

I also received the gift of writing guidance from many. Rachel Newman, my first mentor and proprietor of Lazarus Tribe Media, gave me the gift of writing freedom. She took my training for writing dense medical notes and encouraged me to unleash the message the Lord gave me. I would not be where I am without her.

I joined a few mentoring groups for Christian writers in my quest to grow in the craft. I am indebted to The FlourishWriters Academy and Compel Training. I want to thank Mindy Kiker and Jennifer Kochert for the gift of mentoring wisdom. The Academy came with mentoring calls, and let me tell you, these women are part of the flourish that grew this book into a polished state.

I also have extreme gratitude for my friends and writers in two online groups that bless me so much. Shirley, Margaret, Camila, Sheila, Nancy, Grace, and Keri Ann from "Compel Training Critique Group 4" gave the gift of editing several chapters of this book and the encouragement to keep going. Marvita, Melissa, Jennifer, Beth, and Tammy from "FlourishWriters Academy Bible Study Mastermind Group 2," gave me the gifts of accountability and fervent prayer. I will always cherish the wisdom I received from the women in these groups to complete this book.

Many thanks to Denise Pass for accepting me as an intern and helping me to realize my love of editing podcasts. I am grateful for the gift of mentoring friendship. She is one of the sweetest ladies on the planet. Thank you as well to my fellow interns: Tabatha, Tonna, Danielle, Claudia, Robin, Shelley, Anne, and Lisa. Their social media feedback has been stellar! Thank you to Sam Dovel and Gabrial Hogan at Your Mission Media for the gift of my gorgeous website.

A shout of gratitude to my fellow writer and BFF Kelly Wilbanks. I knew I found a friend when I spied her collection of international Starbucks mugs prominently displayed in her kitchen. The gifts she gives me seem to never cease.

A hearty "toda raba" to the people who influenced my time in Israel, bringing the Bible to life in a way I could have never imagined until I decided to go. Lysa TerKeurst ignited my desire to go with her picture devotional blogs after her first trip there. I'm extremely thankful for my first tour, which she led with staff from Proverbs 31 a few years later. A great shalom for "Doreen Dove" Levy, my guide on the red bus as well as my second tour in her white Prius. I will take the memory of her astonished response to the dove dive-bombing incident on the Jordan River with me into eternity.

Thank you to Kristin St. Martin, my Bible study table leader and treasured friend. Our time in Israel together was beyond priceless, a true gift, and I can't wait to go again. I'm also thankful for the ultimate mom-mentor and fellow Israel sojourner, Ilene Gerardi, for championing this message and her keen insights about Mt. Arbel.

Special thanks to my Hebrew teachers, Chana and Miri, for the gift of helping me understand a very challenging language. I would not understand the Bible as thoroughly without the gift of their proficient and wonderful teaching.

Many, many thanks to Nate Wright, Matt Cobb, Zac Clark, Anders Clark, and Jeff Kerns for their gift of insightful feedback. These men are my pastors at Memorial Bible Church who so kindly provided theological review for this book. Thank you also to Teresa Coscarart, our Women's Ministry director. Her love of deep dive Bible Studies and prayer has helped shape the writer I am today.

Thank you to my editor, Kate Motaung. Every writer needs people willing to comb through their words with fine-toothed detail and save them from inevitable criticism. Kate lives out her calling well and gave me the gift of a well-combed manuscript.

The gift of beauty in this book is from Nelly Murariu at PixBeeDesign. She designed the cover and formatted its contents. I'm sincerely delighted by how lovely this book is to look at; it is all her.

I am so thankful for the wonderful support of women who read my words on the Peacock Sojourning blog. Much gratitude is due in particular to a Facebook group of 100+ women who read and interacted with the first draft of this book in December 2019. They gifted me with knowledge that I crafted something spiritually meaningful for the Christmas season. They gave me hope that people would one day hold this book in their hands.

Lastly, I am grateful for you, my dear reader. You have gifted my words with an audience, making you a treasured part of this story.

Endnotes

DECEMBER 1

1   A Day in the Life of the Holy Temple - Part I. (2020, March 16). Retrieved July 25, 2020, from https://templeinstitute.org/a-day-in-the-life-of-the-holy-temple-part-1/

2   Dobson, K. (2014). Luke 1.8 Zechariah's division. In *NIV First-Century Study Bible: Explore Scripture in its Jewish and Early Christian Context* (p. 1287). Grand Rapids, MI: Zondervan.

3   A Day in the Life of the Holy Temple - Part 7. (2020, March 16). Retrieved July 25, 2020, from https://templeinstitute.org/a-day-in-the-life-of-the-holy-temple-part-7/

4   ibid.

DECEMBER 2

5   Henry, M. (2009). Genesis 3: Verses 14-15. In *Matthew Henry's Commentary on the Whole Bible (Concise)*. Peabody, MA: Hendrickson. Retrieved from https://biblestudytools.com/commentaries/matthew-henry-concise/genesis/3.html

6   Luke 3 and Matthew 1

7   Micah 5:2, ESV

8   Rydelnik, M., & Vanlaningham, M. G. (2014). Commentary on Isaiah 1. The Messianic Sign of Immanuel: His Birth (7:1-16). In *The Moody Bible Commentary* (p. 1020). Chicago, IL: Moody.

9   Richardson, C. C. (1975). In Defense of the Faith: The First Apology of Justin, the Martyr. In *Early Christian Fathers*. New York. Retrieved from https://biblehub.com/library/richardson/early_christian_fathers/the_first_apology_of_justin.htm

DECEMBER 3

10   John 18:13

11   Matthew 3:15, ESV

DECEMBER 5

12   Leviticus 13:45

13   Gillen, D. (2007, June 10). Biblical Leprosy: Shedding Light on the Disease that Shuns. Retrieved from https://answersingenesis.org/biology/disease/biblical-leprosy-shedding-light-on-the-disease-that-shuns/

14   Luke 5:12b, ESV

15   Ellicot, C. J. (n.d.). Ellicot's Commentary for English Readers. Retrieved from https://biblehub.com/commentaries/ellicott/leviticus/14.htm

16   Gill, J. (1976). Luke 5:12. In *Exposition of the Old and New Testament*. Streamwood, IL: Primitive Baptist Library. Retrieved from https://www.biblestudytools.com/commentaries/gills-exposition-of-the-bible/luke-5-12.html

DECEMBER 6

17   Luke 6:17-19

DECEMBER 7

18   The Editors of Encyclopaedia Britannica. (1998, July 20). Centurion. Retrieved from https://www.britannica.com/topic/centurion-Roman-military-officer

19   Peterson, E. H. (2004). Luke 7:37. In *Message//Remix* (p. 1519). Colorado Springs, CO: Nav-Press Publishing Group.

20   Society, E. B. (2014). Luke 7:37. In *The Voice Reader's Bible* (p. 769). Nashville, TN: Thomas Nelson.

21   Strong, J. (1983). 1135. guné. In Strong's Exhaustive Concordance: Showing every word of the text of the common English version of the canonical books, and every occurrence of each word in regular order, together with dictionaries of the Hebrew and Greek words of the original, with refer-ences to the English words. Grand Rapids, MI: Baker Book House. Retrieved from https://www.biblehub.com/greek/1135.htm

22   Souter, A. (1917). *A Pocket Lexicon to the Greek New Testament* (p. 14). Oxford: Clarendon Press.

DECEMBER 8

23   Luke 22:42b, ESV

24   Mark 5:25

25   Mark 5:28, ESV

26   Luke 8:45, ESV

27   Malachi 4:2, ESV

28   Dobson, K. (2014). Luke 8:44 The Edge of His Cloak. In NIV First-Century Study Bible: Explore Scripture in its Jewish and Early Christian Context (p. 1305). Grand Rapids, MI: Zondervan.

DECEMBER 10

29   Strong, J. (1926). 3869. *parakathizo*. In Strong's Exhaustive Concordance: Showing every word of the text of the common English version of the canonical books, and every occurrence of each word in regular order, together with A Comparative Concordance of the Authorized and Revised Versions, including the American Variations; also brief dictionaries of the Hebrew and Greek words of the original with references to the English words. New York: The Methodist Book Con-cern. doi:https://biblehub.com/str/greek/3869.htm

30   Vamosh, M. F. (2008). Women's Worship in the Second Temple. In Women at the Time of the Bible (p. 58). Nashville, TN: Abingdon Press.

31   Souter, A. (1917). A Pocket Lexicon to the Greek New Testament (p. 201). Oxford: Clarendon Press.

32   ibid.

33   ibid.

34   ibid.

35   ibid.

36   Higgs, Liz Curtis. "Word by Word: Martha." Podcast. 2018. https://podcasts.apple.com/us/podcast/word-by-word-martha/id1333168701?i=1000404687000

37   John 11:21, ESV

38   John 11:25-26, ESV

39   John 11:27, ESV

DECEMBER 12

40   Easton, M.G. (1897). Swallow. In Illustrated Bible Dictionary, Third Edition. Edinburgh, Scot-land: Thomas Nelson. Retrieved from https://biblestudytools.com/dictionaries/eastons-bible-dictionary/swallow.html

DECEMBER 14

41 Currid, J. D., & Chapman, D. W. (2016). Leviticus 2:13 salt. In ESV Archaeology Study Bible: English Standard Version (p. 151). Wheaton, IL: Crossway Books.

42 Matthew 5:13

43 Luke 14:34 and Mark 9:50

DECEMBER 15

44 van Rijn, Rembrandt. 1669. The Return of the Prodigal Son. [Oil on canvas.] St. Petersburg: The Hermitage State Museum. Reproduction license purchased from Scala/Art Resource, N.Y.

45 Luke 15:21, ESV

46 Luke 15:32, ESV

DECEMBER 16

47 Souter, A. (1917). A Pocket Lexicon to the Greek New Testament (p. 168). Oxford: Clarendon Press.

48 Psalm 119:105, ESV

49 Psalm 119:24

50 Psalm 119:6

51 Psalm 119:9

52 Psalm 119:37

53 Psalm 119:98

54 Psalm 119:101

55 John 1:29

56 Galatians 5:18, ESV

57 John 14:26

58 John 1:1

59 Galatians 5:14, ESV

DECEMBER 18

60 Luke 18:27, ESV

DECEMBER 19

61 Easton, M. G. (1897). Zacchaeus. In Illustrated Bible Dictionary, Third Edition. Edinburgh, Scotland: Thomas Nelson. Retrieved from https://www.biblegateway.com/resources/eastons-bible-dictionary/Zacchaeus

62 Jastrow, M., Jr., Price, I. M., Jastrow, M., & Kohler, K. (2002). Balsam. Retrieved from http://jewishencyclopedia.com/articles/2415-balsam

63 Jericho: History. (n.d.). Retrieved from https://www.jewishvirtuallibrary.org/jericho

64 Psalm 24:3, ESV

65 Psalm 24:4, ESV

66 Matthew 5:8, ESV

67 Luke 19:8, ESV

68 Luke 19:9

69 Luke 19:20, ESV

70 Psalm 24:5

DECEMBER 20

71 Roy, S. (1986). Cornerstone. In Cambridge English Dictionary. New Delhi: Pankaj. Retrieved from
    https://dictionary.cambridge.org/us/dictionary/english/cornerstone

72 Daniel 2:34

73 Matthew 7:24-26

74 Matthew 21:33

75 Luke 20:16

76 John 15:5

DECEMBER 21

77 Peterson, E. H. (2004). Daniel 12:13. In Message//Remix (p. 1298). Colorado Springs,
    CO: NavPress Publishing Group.

78 Translation, B. E. (1996). Luke 21:36. In Holy Bible, New Living Translation. Wheaton, IL:
    Tyndale House. Retrieved from https://www.biblehub.com/luke/21-36.htm

79 Revelation 21:4

80 Philippians 3:21

81 Isaiah 25:6

82 Currid, J. D., & Chapman, D. W. (2016). Revelation 4:8b. In *ESV Archaeology Study Bible:
    English Standard Version* (p. 1896). Wheaton, IL: Crossway Books.

DECEMBER 22

83 Dobson, K. (2014). Matthew 26:26-30 The Passover Seder. In *NIV First-Century Study Bible:
    Explore Scripture in its Jewish and Early Christian Context* (p. 1237). Grand Rapids, MI: Zondervan.

84 1 Corinthians 11:23-26, ESV

85 1 Corinthians 11:32, ESV

DECEMBER 23

86 Matthew 16:24

About the Author

Jennifer resides in central Washington State. While at times she misses city life, she enjoys the slower pace of rural living. She grew up in Yakima, left to explore the world, and returned in 2005.

Tom is her husband, and her kids are Mitchell, Carol Anne, and Ella Rose. With adult bonus children, grandchildren, and many close relatives in the mix, she delights in her extended-extended family. She also enjoys her church family and serves at Memorial Bible Church in a variety of ways.

Jenni loves hopping on a plane for an adventure. She keeps up to date with Biblical archaeology and strives to learn Hebrew. Viewing art as well as creating it delights her. Historical fiction and memoirs are her favorite book genres, but the Bible is the book that delights her the most.

Spiritually, she is obsessed with all things Jesus. She grew up believing, walked away in college, and re-dedicated her life to Him after going through a divorce. She firmly believes that the Word of God is 100% true.

Her favorite Bible verse is Psalm 91:4, from the Psalm of protection. "He will cover you with his feathers, and under his wings you will find refuge; his faithfulness will be your shield and rampart." (NIV) She loves that God uses a soft, delicate feather to demonstrate to us His protective, sheltering power. She discovered that tucked under the tender wings of God is the safest place to be.

She began writing after going to Israel for the first time in 2015. The Bible suddenly was rich with colors, tastes, and smells. As she flew home, she started writing down the story of her transformation in the Holy Land. She continued this practice after her visit to Rome and Greece to study Biblical history in 2017 and a second trip to Israel in 2018. Covid disrupted a self-guided family trip, and she plans to make that up as soon as possible! Perhaps, one day, her dream of leading a Bible study tour to the Holy Land will become reality—and you can come too.

You can find her at *www.jenniferelwood.com* where her blog, Peacock Sojourning, resides amongst other endeavors. On Facebook, her official page is Jennifer Elwood, Author (*https://www.facebook.com/peacocksojourning*). On Instagram, she is @peacocksojourning (*https://www.instagram.com/peacocksojourning/*). She also began dabbling in Pinterest, at *https://www.pinterest.com/peacocksojourning/*.

Made in the USA
Middletown, DE
06 December 2020